CREATING
HOLY
SPACES

Also by Delia Halverson:

Ready, Set, Teach! Training and Supporting Volunteers in Christian Education

Children's Activities for the Christian Year

Teaching the Lord's Prayer

Teaching Prayer in the Classroom: Experiences for Children and Youth (Revised Edition)

Side by Side: Families Learning and Living the Faith Together

DELIA HALVERSON
KAREN APPLEBY

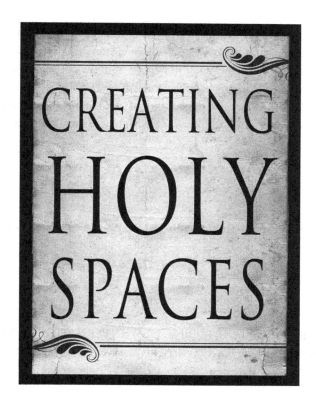

CREATING HOLY SPACES

WORSHIP VISUALS FOR THE REVISED COMMON LECTIONARY

Abingdon Press
Nashville

CREATING HOLY SPACES
WORSHIP VISUALS FOR THE REVISED COMMON LECTIONARY

This book is printed on acid-free paper.

Library of Congress Cataloging-in-Publication Data has been requested.

ISBN   978-1-4267-5479-1

12 13 14 15 16 17 18 19 20 21—10 9 8 7 6 5 4 3 2 1

MANUFACTURED IN THE UNITED STATES OF AMERICA

CONTENTS

CONTENTS

INTRODUCTION

With excitement I went to a conference weekend event, expecting great worship experiences along with learning and networking among other church leaders. At this annual affair, each year worship seemed more meaningful to me than it had the past year. This year a new team planned worship. After the first worship service I knew something was missing. Yet all around me I heard others comment on how the service had enriched their experience with God. What was wrong with me? In conversation with another person who felt the same way, we realized that we missed the visuals of previous years. She and I are both visual persons, and the leaders of that year's worship leaned to the audio expressions of worship. The service lacked a balance. We who worshiped best through visuals had no connection to the theme or to the message.

That was many years ago, and since then I have become more and more aware of the importance of some sort of visual focus in our worship. I recognized this even in my personal worship. Something as simple as moving my devotional time to the porch where I could look out on God's world made a difference. And so I felt God calling me to write another book, one that would help leaders develop visuals to balance the audio in worship.

I had experienced retreats led by Karen Appleby and networked with her over the years, and so I asked her to team with me in this venture. I hope you will find the suggestions that she and I bring to you as exciting as we have found them in writing this book. Blessings to you as you allow the Holy Spirit to work through you in your ministry.

—Delia Halverson

www.deliahalverson.com

www.deliahalverson.blogspot.com

Fifteen years ago while finishing my seminary studies at St. Paul School of Theology, I was asked to create a Krasny Ugol in my home to use as a place of prayer and meditation during the semester. The literal translation for *Krasny Ugol* is "red corner," but it means "beautiful corner" in the life of the Orthodox Christian home. It is a special, spiritual place in the home to give thanks, seek guidance, and invoke blessings. We were taught that how the space is set up visually is important. It was that assignment that first made me realize the connection we can strengthen with God when we use the visual.

I spent my twenty-five years in ministry serving as a Christian educator, church consultant, foundation director, and associate pastor in five different churches across the country. I have enjoyed the variety of ministry settings and the people I met. From the very beginning my friend and mentor was Delia Halverson. Even with miles between us, I knew I could always call her for advice, inspiration, and friendship. How delighted I was when she asked me to work on this book with her.

I hope you will receive ideas for your own worship spaces. They may be in your home, at a retreat location, or in your local church. Even more, I hope your own creative ideas will spring forth in spirit and awe. May you and others experience God in new ways in our ever-revealing creation.

—Karen Appleby

Creating Holy Spaces Digital Edition

Those who purchase *Creating Holy Spaces* have access to the digital edition of the book, found at www.abingdonpress.com/creatingholyspaces. When you visit the site, please click on the link to the digital edition, and when prompted enter the following password: **holyspaces2012**. The web page will provide instructions on either viewing the digital edition in your browser, or downloading it to your own computer. In addition to the full text of the book, the digital edition provides access to full-sized electronic files of the worship visuals that appear in thumbnail size throughout the print edition. **Please note:** When you see one of these thumbnails in the print edition that says "Online Image," it means that the worship visual in question is available only in the digital edition.

CHAPTER 1

WHY A SPIRITUAL, VISUAL SPACE

This book is an ideas book, a helps book, a springboard, and a place to begin. It can help you tap into the creative nature that God gave each of us. This book can be used by pastors, worship leaders and teams, retreat leaders, and teachers, and for personal use in creating a worship or devotion space in a home.

We compiled this book for leaders and readers interested in following the liturgical year and its readings; however, you do not have to follow it using the lectionary. The scripture and topical indexes at the back will help you use the suggestions at any time. We offer suggestions and ideas for bringing a visual dimension into the worship experience.

The primary purpose of this book is to lift up the following ways of augmenting worship:

- Using the visual to enhance the experience of God's presence, worship, and prayer;
- Adding a multifaceted dimension to the worship time;
- Helping guide people on the focus of the message, scripture, or theme;
- Connecting devotion to words, music, prayer, and Eucharistic times; and
- Helping everyone worship God in a more intentional way.

Liturgy means the work of the people. And as Thomas Aquinas stated, liturgy is for the people, not for God. Worship is like a drama: the leaders are the prompters, the people are the actors, and God is the audience. We want to make the best effort of our work and time as we prepare to come together to worship and praise God. The visual arts can be just as helpful as the music we use and the songs we sing. Visual arts deepen our experiences and understandings. Visuals bring forth our cultures, time, and elements of tradition. From the very beginning, Christians used the visual to tell the stories, share the heart, and express the connections we have with God and with each other. In fact, churches originally installed stained-glass windows to help those who could not read or remember the stories. Liturgical space theology is the use of space for transformation and for the growth in relationship with God that can happen in that space.

Personalities and Worship

We now realize that our personalities make a difference in the acts and procedures that enhance our worship. We find that some older adults prefer a service with more energy and physical expression, what we now call contemporary worship. We also see some teens and young adults who prefer a more liturgical service. We often overlook a third type of worship, a contemplative worship that has periods of silence and reflection. We all need, at times, to experience all three styles of worship, but our personalities lead us to one more than another.

In exploring some of the Myers-Briggs personality types, we find that visuals help us, no matter our personality. We give you some suggestions for this below. For more information on spirituality and personality types, we suggest two books: *Knowing Me, Knowing God* by Malcolm Goldsmith and *Discover Your Spiritual Type* by Corinne Ware.

Introverts and Extroverts

We gain energy in different ways. Extroverts gain energy from people and activity, and introverts gain energy from quiet, reflective times. Visuals can appeal to both introverts and extroverts. The extrovert will see the visual as an exciting way to understand the theme or message. The introvert will take the visual into his or her heart and mull it over throughout the worship time.

Sensers and Intuitives

Sensers take in information through the senses, and the visual images bring the theme home to them. They also benefit from touch, smell, and taste. Even when those senses are not used, the visual can help them imagine the roughness of a rugged cross or the smell of a bottle of perfumed oil or the taste of a fruit.

Intuitives take in information through imagination. They will use the visual as a stepping stone into imagining the theme or understanding the passage of scripture. Since intuitives quickly become bored with repetition, the freshness of a new visual for each service will enhance their worship. They find that words cannot describe God, and so the visuals add a dimension to their experience.

Thinkers and Feelers

We all are thinkers and feelers to some degree, but some personalities thrive more on thinking and others more on expressing their feelings. Thinkers enjoy an order in their worship experience. Since the very process of thinking can be a form of spiritual exercise to them, a visual in worship gives them opportunity to think about the theme or scripture. These thoughts can be an actual offering to God for thinkers.

Feelers place themselves in other people's shoes. Visuals help them identify with situations and circumstances. A hammer and three nails can help them understand the pain and agony of the crucifixion. They also like peace and harmony, and will often avoid conflict. Sometimes a visual can help them face facts about our world and bring them to action.

Learning Preferences and Worship

Just as we have different personalities, we have different ways of learning. In Matthew 22:7, we hear Jesus telling us to love God with our heart, soul, and mind. Jesus did not separate the mind from worshiping God, and we must take the different ways of learning into account as we prepare worship experiences.

Some of us are more oriented to what we hear, while others are more oriented to what we see. Today's churches lean heavily on the audio, focusing on music and the spoken word. We have a mission to help people who learn more through visuals. For a visual person, a service that has no visual connection can be as meaningless as a service without words or music would be to a person primarily focused on hearing.

Howard Gardner, an authority in brain research, identified eight intelligences that God gave each of us. We all use these intelligences, but each one of us will favor some more than others. Recognizing these intelligences can help enhance our worship time.

- Jesus approached his verbal/linguistic followers with the use of stories and scripture. Visuals can act as a bridge between the words and the listener.
- Jesus often used questions and answers to provoke the logical/mathematical follower into thinking and reasoning. A visual can trigger questioning thoughts for this type of learner.
- Jesus used common objects as he explained his meanings to the visual/spatial follower. In the following pages we offer a rich supply of suggestions for such common objects. The way that you set up your focal center makes a difference here too.
- Jesus involved his body/kinesthetic learners by taking them fishing and washing their feet. Although visuals do not always involve movement, they can often trigger thoughts of movement for worshipers.
- Jesus and his disciples often sang hymns. Other types of music were common in the worship of that day. We usually involve some form of music in our worship experiences, and simply placing musical instruments or musical notes in the worship space can often connect the musical/rhythmic learner to the message.
- Jesus developed small groups and other opportunities for his interpersonal followers. When we all view the same visual, we can feel connected to others in our worshiping community.
- Jesus drew himself and his disciples aside for intrapersonal reflection. Visuals in the worship time draw us to reflect within ourselves, an experience that people today have very little opportunity to explore.
- Jesus used nature as illustrations and even taught outside. When we bring nature into the worship area, we help each person worship through God's world.

CHAPTER 2

THE LECTIONARY AND CHRISTIAN SEASONS

What is the lectionary? The Revised Common Lectionary is a three-year cycle of scripture readings used as a worship guide by more than twenty denominations. One great advantage to using the lectionary is the way it brings a comprehensive scope, an interesting variety, and an overview of the Bible coordinated to the seasons of the church. It also gives a balance of different Scriptures such as the Hebrew texts, the Psalms, the Gospels, the Letters, and other good news books. Without such a guide, we could easily fall into a rut of using our own favorite Scriptures and miss the richness that other readings bring to the worship experience.

The seasons of the Christian year create a rhythm that helps us remember the life of Christ. Instead of looking at the seasons as repetitive events that occur year after year, we must begin seeing the year as a flow through our contemporary lives, a living out of the faith story each year. Built into these seasons are special things that we do and see and hear, even things that we smell and touch that awaken our senses to seeing Christ anew all around us.

Season	Time	Color	Symbols
Advent (*from the Latin word for "coming" adventus*)	Four Sundays before and up to Christmas	purple (*royalty*) or blue (*Mary's color—hope*)	wreath (*God's eternal love*) evergreens (*ever-living*) candle (*Christ as light of world*) trumpets (*prophecy*) Jesse tree (*symbols of Jesus' ancestors, see Isaiah 11:1*)
Christmas	Christmas Eve and 12 days after, to Epiphany	white (*coming of light*)	Chrismon tree nativity scene angels Christmas star poinsettia, rose
Epiphany	January 6	white and gold	three crowns (*Note: number of kings is not biblical but traditional*) three gifts Christmas star
Season after Epiphany	Days between Jan. 6 and Ash Wednesday	1st and last Sundays—white; others—green	baptismal font, shell (*Jesus' baptism*) water jars (*miracle at Cana*) green plant (*life/ ministry of Christ*)

Season	Time	Color	Symbols
Lent	Ash Wednesday to Easter	purple *(royalty, penitence)*	rough cross veil over cross remove shiny objects and flowers
Holy Week	Week before Easter Palm Sunday Maundy Thursday Good Friday	purple or red black *(darkness)*	coins, whip, crown of thorns, and so forth palm branches grapes, bread, chalice, foot-washing cross draped black—no altar cloths
Easter	Easter Sunday to Pentecost	white, gold, and festive colors	Flowers *(particularly those grown from dried "dead" bulbs)* empty cross/tomb butterfly and cocoon peacock *(sheds and regrows feathers)* phoenix *(mythical bird rose from ashes)*

Season	Time	Color	Symbols
Pentecost	50th day after Easter	red (*fire or the Holy Spirit*)	flame of fire doves red flowers ship (*church as ship*) rainbow
Season after Pentecost	Day after Pentecost to Advent	green (*growth in Christ*)	triangle (*on Trinity Sunday*) green plant

(Some churches choose to extend the Pentecost Season, celebrating outreach to people of all nations as they remember the gift of languages at Pentecost. See Acts 2.)[1]

You will find more suggestions for traditional symbols and props in the appendix on pages 159-63. The book *Teaching & Celebrating the Christian Seasons*, by Delia Halverson, will give you more background on the particular seasons.

Note

1. Delia Halverson, *Nuts & Bolts of Christian Education* (Nashville: Abingdon Press, 2000), p. 51.

CHAPTER 3

HELPS IN CREATING A VISUAL SPACE

L et's get started! Creating a visual space involves more than just throwing some objects on a table. Recognize that you are prompting others to carry out their actions as they actively worship our awesome God. You are an agent of God, allowing the Holy Spirit to work through you. We find it helpful to bless the space. A blessing comes about in prayers of thanksgiving for God's presence and prayers for God's guidance as we plan the creation and setup. There is no mistake in the construction that God brings about. The time we have with God in making the display is co-creation. The insights that we receive are wonderful gifts. What others do or do not receive in the vignette is not our responsibility. Any holy and spiritual space is an experience between the Creator of all and the one who waits and watches. The messages and insights are their own. The Spirit moves as it may. Be open in your creating and in your observation.

Creating a Visual Display

We suggest that displays in a sanctuary change weekly, centering on a theme or the liturgical readings. But also consider seasons or groups of worship experiences that have a theme running through them. During Lent or Advent, you may create a display as the basic prop for all the Sundays of that season. Then the only changes made each individual day or Sunday would be the adornments or smaller symbols on it. During Advent, for example, an evergreen bough might be placed on a display, and each week you would simply add different symbols representing the shepherds, angels, and so forth.

For a retreat, the focus display table might have the overall visual based on the theme and purpose of the retreat. Then at each session, add something to represent the focus of that session. We have used bare tree branches on a table and hung representative symbols and items throughout a retreat weekend. We have also asked participants to bring or collect and display their own symbols and items as part of the opening and closing moments of a retreat. Personal symbols can be very effective.

In the home, create a prayer corner to display items that change monthly or seasonally depending on the time of year. In this worship space, you might also focus on where you are in your journey or time in your life. Use visuals in your worship as moving devotional tools.

The display area can be symbolic and directive. It can also be interactive. You may use the items on the table as part of the message. For example, if the message includes reference to God's word being as sweet as honey, the display might have pieces of honey candy on it that can later be taken by the congregation and enjoyed. Having a display each week can help the person giving the children's sermon. The items on the table can also serve as the visuals and props that not only keep children's attention but also connect the children's message to the greater theme and scripture of the day.

The display often becomes as exciting as a game. Expectant worshipers come to church in anticipation of what will be displayed this day. And the attention is not lost as people try to recognize the connection between the visual and the message that unfolds. This brings joy for all ages.

The display brings the greatest gift in the way it ties the parts to the whole. Base the work on the Scriptures, tie everything into the greater theme of the day, and be intentional about articulating themes to observers of all ages. And, finally, be part of the creative process yourself. On page 157 of the appendix, you will find a page you can copy and use for your own ideas and notes. A sample of the note card appears on the page opposite this one.

Materials

Wouldn't it be wonderful to have a studio full of all the materials you need to create spiritual displays? Some of us are so lucky. There may be spaces, closets, or unoccupied rooms where we can organize and save items that can be used each week. Some of us may resort to an old trunk, cellar, or attic. Some of us may have multiple places where items can

My Notes
A-ha Ideas:
Supplies to Collect:
Date Used:

be collected and saved. The key is to have an organized way of listing what you want to use, where it is, and how to get it.

Start with a basic collection of arts and crafts supplies. Most items we can readily find around us. Some may be borrowed or just moved from one place to another. Keep a running list of wonderful pieces you know about, the person who owns them, and the way to reach that person. If you anticipate needing an object, send out a message to persons in your congregation ahead of time, asking them if they have such an object. Having their personal item used in the display will bring even more meaning to their worship experience. Take care and return the item promptly. Also keep a record so that you know where to find it should you want to use it again. Of course, you may need to buy other materials. Anything from a beautiful prop or statue to basic paper, fabrics, or markers will come in handy. Look around. You will find so much right in your midst that can be used. Keep good records of their whereabouts. On page 158 of the appendix you will find a form to copy and use. Or you can set up such a form on your computer.

Collect items and symbols as you come across them. Objects have meaning beyond themselves. Jesus emphasized his message with the use of parables each time using ordinary stories of people and situations to tell his own story and teach a message. We, like Jesus, can use ordinary symbols and objects to express "the more."

We have included a list of some items on pages 159-63 in the appendix for starters. These suggestions are just a beginning to the multitude of ideas you will come up with on your own. Make use of what you find in your midst. Also consider recycling and reusing materials. It is a great, green thing to do.

Help from the Village

You do not have to create displays all by yourself. You may want to organize a team of people to help. Artistic, creative friends can help in the most amazing ways. The fun and fellowship that comes when working together is a testament to the energy that community fosters. Impress on your team that you are not just creating a display but a means to lead worshipers to a richer relationship with God. When you begin to create your visual, take a moment for prayer and ask God to guide you as you plan and work.

Other suggestions include asking a class of children to make something that can be displayed. One year we asked the children to create bells out of different colors of construction paper. We suspended them from the sanctuary ceiling with names of church members who had passed away the previous year printed on them. They floated gently in the air on All Saints Sunday in memory of our departed loved ones. And the children were so happy to have their creations used in church. (If your ceilings are too high, you might hang them from a cross bar on standards that are brought to the front and placed in holders.)

And, of course, there are the artists in our midst. Use their God-given talents in a multitude of ways. Quilters, sewers, painters, calligraphers, photographers, and sculptors are usually happy to lend their creations on any given day. Again the key is to keep a descriptive list of items and artists to call at the right time. If you ask them to create something special, be sure to give them plenty of time to do so. You might also give them credit for their creation in the bulletin—not in the order of worship but in another spot in the bulletin.

Centering

A visual space not only helps direct and focus our thoughts but also clears and opens the mind. When we arrive at church on Sunday morning, at a retreat place, or at a time of devotion in our own homes, our minds are filled with distractions. Just when we want to quiet ourselves to God, we wander off to past reflections, plans of future responsibilities, and present concerns.

We know that there are prayer types and spiritual discipline practices that can help bring us to God. This book includes and focuses on how the visual helps us center on the word of God. Creating a spiritual display or space is a discipline in itself. Displays and vignettes can take snapshots from the biblical story, hint ideas to contemplate from spiritual themes, and direct the thoughts of our minds in specific ways. But, more important, they can help us release the noise and racing in our minds. Visuals can open up thin places and free up realms for God to speak and connect. Just as an icon of old or a Mandela image of today creates pause, a visual display can give us freedom with God.

Remember that the material items and props are only part of the space. Are there objects that distract from the focus of the worship time? We often focus mainly on a display. But in planning, remember that the air space around the display is also very important. Pray for the nothingness in its midst to speak to each person. The visual display hints; the accompanying space is God's place to speak.

Symbolism

There are levels of symbolism. Our displays may portray the exact story or theme of the day. We would encourage that, on occasion, the display be more vague and mysterious. This gives the observer more freedom to receive spiritual messages within the mystery. Or, for the more analytical observer, the mind stays focused in the space and pursues the connection from the artistry to the message. Sometimes, use symbols that are not so obvious. Embrace the mystery. You will find a list of traditional symbols and contemporary symbols or props in appendix 3.

Symbols are not deeply explained by words but are more suggestive and open to the mysteries shared between God and the observer. Symbols become metaphoric. They provide open space and thin places for the Spirit to work. Though a symbol might directly represent a story, verse, or experience, it also can mean more. Symbols open up contemplation on the meaning for each of us today. They awaken the imagination, the questions, and the relationship with our God. Displays, like the spirit, need to offer openness beyond literalism.

Elements of Design

The elements of design include line, form, texture, color, composition, and space. Variety is good. So is learning how to use each element artfully. Collect very basic art books on the elements of design. Become familiar with the elements, and use books to help your creativity grow. The information in them will be helpful and inspiring. Let us look briefly at some of the elements:

Line: Look at the lines in your composition. Remember that some lines—such as spirals, circles, rays, and upward lines—have spiritual representations.

Form and Texture: The use of curves, natural materials, and symbols from nature (such as orbs, celestial shapes, growing plants, water, grasses, seeds, and soils) all are examples of form and textures you can include.

Color: Besides the colors that are assigned to the Christian year, colors also represent and evoke emotions and feelings. Consider this list of colors and their characters:

White and gold	joy, festivity, peace, pardon, unity
Grey and black	humility, guilt, death, sadness, the unknown
Brown	support, grounding, earth, the ability to produce
Purple	penitence, dignity, strength, royalty, spirituality, inspiration, leadership
Red	fire, Holy Spirit, passion, creation
Blue	truth, right spirit, clarity, communication, peace, trust, creativity, innovation
Green	growth, hope, renewal, rebirth, healing, balance, prosperity, harmony, generosity
Yellow	happiness, cheerfulness, intelligence, purity
Orange	energy, life, success, pride, joy, vitality

Space: Sacred space is more than three dimensional. There is a fourth dimension. Some call it God space. As you design your vignette, let God fill the space. Feel the spirit that comes with the creating. Gertrud Nelson said it best in *To Dance with God:* "Sacred space is not practical space. It is enclosed and set apart for the transcendent."[1]

Composition: A very important point to keep in mind is to see your composition as the most important element in this work. Remember these three things: tell a story, keep it simple, and have a focal point.

The advantage of using the lectionary is the design around the church year. Each denomination and church follows its own traditions, but traditional seasons and colors on the chart in chapter 2 can be used in the display as well.

Know Your Space

Step back and consider the whole worship space. Your display rests within a larger context. What are the other colors you see? Are there paraments on display? What is the color of the liturgical season? What fabrics, paintings, stained-glass windows, or other colorful items might you play off of or coordinate with? How can your display flow within the greater space? Or, is there a good reason to have the display shockingly different than the rest? So that a display is more easily seen, consider light objects against dark backdrops and dark objects against light backdrops. Set objects at different heights to add variety.

In a sanctuary or worship space, there are up to seven sub-spaces that have a flow between them. Your display may be located in just one of them, but be aware of how all the spaces connect. Identify the gathering spaces, and notice the spaces that involve movement. The gathered people worship together in the congregational space. Be aware of where the choirs, instruments, and other music-related activities are set. Where do you usually place the altar and table? Is there a permanent baptismal space? And consider the locations of the pulpit and lecterns. If possible, place your display area near the lectern so that the eye moves easily between the liturgical reader or person giving the message and the visual.

Scale and Size

Worship spaces come in many varieties. There are different styles, sizes, shapes, and ages. Consider the area that surrounds your visual display. Take into consideration the size of the worship space as well as the scale of your space to the full worship area. With a wide worship space, consider having two displays—one on either side. If the worship space is deep, place the displays forward, and even place one midway down the aisle so those seated in the back have a better view. If your service includes projected graphics, consider photographing and projecting your display on the screen for all to see.

Most important is the spiritual dimension of the space. Become familiar with Celtic Christianity and the scripture from Acts (17:28) that states, "in him we live and move and have our being." The display is larger than the space it takes up. The spirit moves around the visual, out and between the art itself and the observer.

Multiples

How can we emphasize the significance of smaller objects? Consider all the symbolism we find in items such as seeds, shells, bird's nests, and coins. Think about using many of the same items when they are small, even if it requires hundreds to make it more effective. Not only can you place these in abundance on the display area, but you may scatter them throughout the room. For example, if a display features seashells, scatter some on windowsills, tables, and entrance areas as well. String single shells on a string or ribbon for the ushers and greeters to wear around their necks that day, or give each person a small shell as he or she enters the worship area. Request to have a shell sketch used on the bulletin cover or in projected displays.

Materials

Start collecting, saving, and storing. In appendix 3 of this book is a list of both traditional and more modern symbols and items that would be good to collect or note where they can be retrieved. You will use some items often over time. Here are just a few of the basic building blocks:

- Candles and holders
- Crosses
- Vases, pots, and florist supplies
- Stands and easels of many sizes
- Rocks, stones, bare branches, pieces of wood
- Cloth of different colors and textures

- Extension cord or power supply for times you may want electricity
- Baskets and plastic fruits and vegetables

See a list of more ideas in the appendix, pages 159-63.

Ready, Set, Go

Planning Together

Communicate with the worship leaders and the preacher or speaker. Having the overall theme permeate throughout the worship time is wonderful. Coordinating the message, music, readings, printed materials, and visuals makes for a complete plan.

Helpful considerations:
1. What Scriptures are in the lectionary this day?
2. Which Scripture in particular will the message or music or season lift up?
3. What one symbol or image best represents the overall theme?
4. Which modern-day stories or symbols are representative?
5. Is this day part of a series? Can you use the basis of the display for consecutive days with different parts changed out weekly?

In his book *To Crown the Year*, Peter Mazar suggests four principles to planning spiritual space.
1. That the space within the space needs to have a fit location.
2. That there is a climate of hospitality inviting the observer into the space.
3. That the images are appropriate, directing, suggestive, and open to individual reflection.
4. In community, that tradition is honored and respected.[2]

Creation Time

- Take time for your idea to come together. Based on prayer, conversation, use of this book, and study of the Scripture, have your plan in mind.
- Generate the list of supplies and materials you will need and have them ready to go.
- Choose and schedule the time when you will put it together. Make sure the sanctuary or worship space is available when you want to work on it. And make arrangements to leave it up if the area is shared space. You do not want another group moving your display and leaving you any surprises.

- Allow enough time for your work. Give yourself enough extra time to make this a devotional time for yourself or those who are helping you when you are finished. In this ministry, the development of the inner space, that of the heart and soul, holds primary importance. Allow yourself to receive the gift you are giving to others.
- Make notes to save for future reference. Record the date and place. Sometimes the best inspiration for the next project comes from the one you just finished.
- Take a picture of the display to keep with your notes.
- Know when you need to disassemble. Take down, return, store, and rejoice!
- Enjoy your prayer time, planning, creating, devotion, and worship time with God. Open your eyes!

Psalm 84

"Even the wren finds a house and the sparrow a nest for herself. Take me home, Lord; guide me to the place of perfect repose. Let me feel you always within me; open my eyes to your love."[3]

Notes

1. Gertrud Nelson, *To Dance with God* (Mahwah, N.J.: Paulist Press, 1986), p. 27.

2. Peter Mazar, *To Crown the Year: Decorating the Church through the Seasons* (Chicago: Liturgy Training Publications, 1995), pp. 2-8.

3. Steven Mitchell, *A Book of Psalms: Selected and Adapted from the Hebrew* (New York: Harper Perennial, 1994), p. 37.

YEAR A

ADVENT

We wait expectantly, "God with us," new beginnings, new life, renewal, get ready. Now is the time to be awake. Be expectant in this amazing time. Prepare, wait, and watch. Now is the time of peace. Now is the time to put on the light. We use purple or blue colors during this season, representing royalty. Purple cloth was very expensive because it took thousands of tiny murex shells to extract just a small amount of dye.

First Sunday of Advent

Isaiah 2:1-5 and Psalm 122	Both of the Old Testament texts have a definite theme of peace. Peace signs can vary from one large or several small signs. Since this is the first Sunday of Advent, we recommend that evergreens (symbolizing God's everlasting love) in a sprig or wreath be used throughout Advent on your display. And, for this first week, adorn it with signs of peace.
Romans 13:11-14	To call attention to the calling forth of light, we suggest a multi-grouping of candles or tea lights throughout the evergreens for this reading. Do consider using artificial greenery for safety reasons.

*

Matthew 24:36-44 — Be ready, stay awake! A large, old-fashioned alarm clock or a big bag of coffee beans with a mug, or both, would certainly draw attention to the message for us to stay awake.

Second Sunday of Advent

Isaiah 11:1-10 — Place a wide variety of stuffed animals in the evergreens. Make sure to have both strong, ferocious animals alongside gentle, weak animals. Consider putting a lion and a lamb together prominently centered. If you are not using greenery, place all the animals together in a large basket.

Psalm 72:1-7, 18-19 — The Psalter reading this week centers on righteousness and peace. So, like last week, peace signs can be used. Always remember that good symbols for any Psalter reading can include music symbols such as sheet music, musical notes cut from cardboard, and instruments such as trumpets.

Romans 15:4-13 — Come. This invitation was being extended to the Gentiles in Paul's letter. The word "Come" can be printed on small cards many times and placed in the greenery. The word "Come" can be done in calligraphy on a large flag. Or, on a lighter note, you could use an intersection traffic light with a green light shining or portrayed more brightly than the red and yellow.

*See page 8 for instructions regarding the digital edition of this book, including access to online only images.

Matthew 3:1-12 — The declaration, "Prepare Ye the Way," may be printed, or use calligraphy on a sign of attention. This Gospel reading also speaks of good fruit. Have different fruits displayed in the evergreens or placed in a basket.

Third Sunday of Advent

Color: blue, purple, or pink

Isaiah 35:1-10 — This beloved text is strikingly displayed when a single, vibrant bloom is placed in an area of sand, small gravel and dirt. This display does not work with evergreens if you are using them throughout Advent.

Psalm 146:5-10 or Luke 1:47-55 — Cutting out symbols of song and music from foil can be used either in the greenery or against a black backdrop.

James 5:7-10 — Follow the growing seeds theme and create a display of seed packets, a hoe, and a watering can. These gardening tools can be incorporated in and with the greenery as well.

Matthew 11:2-11 — A crutch or cane simply displayed with a red X cut from red board and placed on it against black fabric is a good reminder of the healing in this story.

Fourth Sunday of Advent

Isaiah 7:10-16 — The Hebrew texts and the Gospel reading this week revolve around one word, one name, one amazing theme . . . Emmanuel. Consider having the name Emmanuel written on a large, wide ribbon and wrap it around the greenery in your display.

Psalm 80:1-7, 17-19	Emmanuel, same as above.
Romans 1:1-7	Forgiveness is the focus on this reading. You may be able to find a print of Rembrandt's "The Prodigal Son" to use. This famous painting expresses forgiveness in an incredible way. You can find the painting at http://www.rembrandtpainting.net/.
Matthew 1:18-25	Emmanuel, same as Hebrew text suggestion.

Christmas Eve

The Scriptures for this day are the same for all three years. All suggestions are placed in Year A. White or gold is the color of this special night. Many symbols can be used to adorn the vignette such as angels, candles, trumpets, and shepherds. Or you may use a modern symbol such as a lighthouse. For a grouping of words, tonight use all the names of Christ as listed in the Isaiah scripture: Wonderful, Counselor, Mighty God, Everlasting Father, and Prince of Peace.

Isaiah 9:2-7	You might simply use a source of light here, or make a creative display of the names of Christ; Wonderful, Counselor, Mighty God, Everlasting Father, Prince of Peace as described above. Verse 4 speaks of the broken rod of the oppressor, offering freedom. If you use this theme, use the background of a purple drape and make a "nest" of the white drape over it. Place the rod that you have broken over the folds of the white drape. This symbolizes our movement from the waiting time to this time of celebrating the one who has come as Savior. Another suggestion is to place some of the above words over a broken rod on the table.

Psalm 96	A globe and a crown make a good combination to visualize this reading. Or glorious symbols of music and song are beautiful tributes to this reading. Using Verses 11 and 12 as the theme here, place two pictures in front of the white drape, one of a forest and one of the sea.
Titus 2:11-14	Symbols of our response to the gift of Christ such as hands in prayer, rejoicing in song or giving through good works would be great. The literal translation of verse 14 in this passage means to actually pay the cost of the release of the prisoner. When using this theme, you might symbolize the fact that Jesus' life and death redeemed us by covering coins with gold foil and then heaping the coins on a white drape. Or cut the letters "SALVATION" out of gold paper and place them on the purple drape.
Luke 2:1-10	This passage heralds in the special event of the season. To emphasize the inclusiveness of Jesus' message and the fact that the announcement came first to those who were considered of a very low class, spread a drape of burlap as the foundation, and then use a white or gold drape. Place angels from different ethnic backgrounds at different heights among the folds of the top drape. For another suggestion, use a fabric drape that is wooly like sheep and place a shepherd's crook across it. This symbolizes the fact that the first to know about Jesus' birth were those of low esteem, rather than the rulers of the land. Or you might just use angels, angels, and more angels.

YEAR A

CHRISTMAS

For the season of Christmas we use the colors of white and gold, signifying purity and royalty. Too often we ignore this season because we have put such emphasis on the Sundays leading up to Christmas. But these should be glorious Sundays of celebration!

Christmas Sunday/Christmas Day

The Scriptures for this day are the same for all three years. All suggestions are placed in Year A.

We use white, yellow, and gold colors for this special day. Symbols include nativities, Chrismons, the Jesse Tree, and light. Consider a grouping of nativity sets collected from the congregation and placed on display. A variety made from wood, porcelain, and even sets made by children make a nice display. Perhaps you can use some from other countries. Place the names of those who contributed to the display in the bulletin. Since the Scriptures are the same for each year, you may want to vary the visual. Or you may establish a traditional visual you will use each year. Some churches have a special crèche that they use. If you will have a service on Christmas morning, use only Mary and Joseph in the crèche and on Christmas morning, add the babe.

Isaiah 52:7-10 and Psalm 98	For these Scriptures that speak of praise, joy, and singing, of ringing out peace, you might drape the table with white and place a mass of ribbons of different colors on the drape. Give each person entering a small bell attached to a ribbon. Then during the service (perhaps during the first hymn) invite them to come forward, ringing their bells and place them on the table.
Hebrews 1:1-12	Both of the New Testament readings evoke images of light. So use an abundance of candle lights to brighten the greenery or any display you create. The passage from Hebrews references things that pass away and the importance of our relationship with God, through Christ, which will go on forever. This might be symbolized by using the manger from a crèche and placing it high with the white drape under it. The circle of a wreath can symbolize how our relationship with God has no end.
John 1:1-14	We speak of the Bible as the Word, and indeed the Gospels are the revelation of this Christ whose birth we celebrate at this time. On a white drape, place the Bible, opened to John 1:1-14, and place a manger piece from a crèche nearby.

First Sunday after Christmas

Isaiah 63:7-9	Add the phrase "Gloria in Excelsis Deo" in calligraphy on a banner.

33

Psalm 148 — To tie into the Psalter reading, place the banner described above next to an ancient style horn. This Scripture is used in the first Sunday after Christmas in years B and C also. Check those suggestions.

Hebrews 2:10-18 — This Scripture speaks of Christ's sacrifice for us and what he took on. During Christmas we think of Jesus as a baby. A display that focuses on the future of this child could be represented with images of the life of Christ from infancy to adulthood.

Matthew 2:13-23 — If you have used nativity figurines on Christmas Eve, take the angel and the figure of Joseph and create a display.

Watch Night/New Year's Eve/New Year's Day

The Scriptures for this day are the same for all three years. All suggestions are placed in Year A.

Ecclesiastes 3:1-13 — "To every season there is a time . . ." A simple display using a clock or a collection of clocks works well for this reading. Or you might use pictures of the four seasons. Search the Web using the phrase "four seasons tree."

Psalm 8 — A mobile of the planets and/or heavenly stars (available on the Internet or at science museums and planetariums) can be hung. The movement of this display makes it especially wonderful. Also consider using a picture of a person looking up into the mass of stars in the sky, recognizing the marvel of God's universe.

Revelation 21:1-6a   This Scripture is appropriate for the ending of the old year and the beginning of the new. Make large symbols of the beginning and ending letters of the Greek alphabet, Alpha and Omega. Or, you may display an image, painting, or print of a sunrise. These tie into the meditation of a new heaven and earth.

Matthew 25:31-46   Any symbols of servant ministry work here. Helping hands, a basin and towel, or images of people helping other people are perfect. You might change this by using one symbol of need and another that offers the help, such as an empty bowl and a bowl with food or a tattered piece of clothing and a nice piece of clothing.

Second Sunday after Christmas

Jeremiah 31:7-14
Psalm 147:12-20
Ephesians 1:3-14   The first three readings this week talk about the gathering of the chosen, the remnant, and God's blessing of the faithful. For a beautiful way to depict these sentiments take a large basket and fill it to the brim and over the sides with fabrics of different colors, textures, and prints.

John 1:(1-9) 10-18   The Gospel reading focuses on grace. This word may be difficult to portray. Try signs of love with hearts or a large glass bowl of chocolate kisses. Ask your preacher where he or she may be going with the message to fine tune the intention.

YEAR A

EPIPHANY

The season of Epiphany deals with the way the magi might have spread the gospel when they returned home and also of Jesus' life. The color for Epiphany is white and then green, starting on the second Sunday after Epiphany.

Epiphany Sunday

The Scriptures for this day are the same for all three years. All suggestions are placed in Year A.

Isaiah 60:1-6
Psalm 72:1-7, 10-14
Ephesians 3:1-12
Matthew 2:1-12

All four readings this week speak to us of gifts. Collect boxes of many shapes and sizes, beautifully gift wrap each of them, and arrange your display. You might also use symbols that represent various talents that God has given us and arrange them for your display. Or you might use the magi from a crèche for this display, since they brought gifts to Jesus.

Baptism of the Lord/First Sunday after the Epiphany

Isaiah 42:1-9 and Psalm 29	Prophesy and the Psalms can be symbolized with a trumpet. The display should be celebratory and unabashedly calling attention to an important announcement. Display a trumpet and perhaps a banner.
Acts 10:34-43	Christ for ALL is the message. Find a large globe, one with a floor stand that sits tall would be perfect. If you set this on a table, use a desktop model.
Matthew 3:13-17	Have the children of the church make doves. There are many simple patterns for making doves out of paper that can be hung from above or placed on display.

Here are some web sites for dove patterns:

http://doingpublicwork.org/
wp-content/uploads/2010/03/
MirandasEasyPaperDoveSmall.pdf

http://tlc.howstuffworks.com/family/how-to-make-easy-christmas-ornaments6.htm (scroll down page)

http://printables.scholastic.com/printables/
detail/?id=30515

YEAR A

ORDINARY TIME (AFTER EPIPHANY)

G reen is the color of this season. Using the word "ordinary" does not mean mundane or common. It comes from the word *ordinal,* which means simply counted or chronological time. In this case, the time in order.

Second Sunday after the Epiphany

Isaiah 49:1-7	In the days of the early Hebrews, Israel was not a country, but a people. To symbolize the chosen people of God, consider using a print or poster of a large gathering of people. Saving posters and illustrations from old curriculum pieces is a great way to have pictures such as this on hand when you need them. You will find *The National Geographic* magazine another good source. Mount the picture and display it on an easel.
Psalm 40:1-11	As before, good symbols for any Psalter reading can include music symbols such as sheet music, musical notes cut from cardboard, and instruments such as trumpets.
1 Corinthians 1:1-9	Strength is a theme here. Consider using a rock to symbolize strength.

John 1:29-42

Since the key word in the Gospel reading is "seeking," it would be fun to use as the modern symbol a floor-standing telescope. Ask around. There are people you may know that have one in their home you can borrow. If not, consider a large magnifying glass.

Third Sunday after the Epiphany

Isaiah 9:1-4 and Psalm 27:1, 4-9

Both Old Testament readings use light. One speaks of light in the darkness and the other of the Lord as the light in its message. A candle or lamp would work. A print or even a model of a lighthouse would also be very effective. Lighthouses are popular subjects for home décor. It shouldn't be too hard to find.

1 Corinthians 1:10-18

"Be not divided, but joined" is a glorious message. Weave many stripes of different fabrics in a variety of colors and textures together in a tapestry and drape it for display.

Matthew 4:12-23

Write the words "Follow me" in various ways and display them on a board. This will simply and effectively depict the Gospel reading of Jesus choosing his disciples and beginning his ministry.

Fourth Sunday after the Epiphany

Micah 6:1-8 and
Psalm 15

These two Scriptures read like a simple check list for righteous living. Consider making a giant checklist out of butcher paper with each of the three ideas written out and a check marked off before each one. Such as:

☑ Do justice

☑ Love kindness

☑ Walk humbly with God

1 Corinthians 1:18-31 and Matthew 5:1-12

In both the New Testament texts we are called forth, even in our foolishness, to be a shining light. The use of lights or candles would make a good symbol.

The Presentation of the Lord/Candlemas

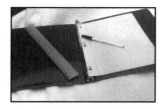

Malachi 3:1-4
Psalm 24
Hebrews 2:14-18
Luke 2:22-40

Spiritual growth takes time, teaching, and guidance from our elders toward maturity. Symbols of adult guidance such as a teacher's ruler or a potter's wheel could be used. And since all these readings lead up to the Gospel story of Jesus' anointing and blessing by Simeon and Anna, a print or icon of this event would be nice.

Fifth Sunday after the Epiphany

Isaiah 58:1-9a
Psalm 112:1-10
1 Corinthians 2:1-12

Both Old Testament texts as well as the verses from Corinthians refer to justice, righteousness, and wisdom. Perhaps you can find a prop or home/office décor item of a weight piece or a scale of justice.

Matthew 5:13-20

The Gospel reading this week is the call for us to be a light and to let our light shine. Again, as so many times, lights, lamps, battery-powered lanterns, candles, or lighthouses are perfect.

Sixth Sunday after the Epiphany

Deuteronomy 30:15-20

The Old Testament reading focuses on choices. Collect a few road signs and display them. Try to find some that have arrows and place them to point in different directions.

Psalm 119:1-8

The Psalter can be depicted by a display of tablets such as the ones people envision when they think of the Ten Commandments.

1 Corinthians 3:1-9

Make a display using soil, pots, seeds, and garden tools to represent spiritual growth.

Matthew 5:21-37

When people look at Rembrandt's painting of *The Prodigal Son*, they think of concepts such as repentance, being sorry, and reconciliation. We suggest this print on different occasions, but it does work very well here. You can find the painting at http://www.rembrandtpainting.net/.

Seventh Sunday after the Epiphany

The overall themes that weave between this week's readings center on the laws, teachings, and foundation of God. If one symbol could be worked for the all readings, consider using several sets of blueprints.

Leviticus 19:1-2, 9-18	Work with homemade scrolls of paper to symbolize the Hebrew laws.
Psalm 119:33-40	This psalm also calls attention to the law. The use of tablets or scrolls works here as well.
1 Corinthians 3:10-11, 16-23	Blueprints are a more modern symbol to symbolize the foundation of God.
Matthew 5:38-48	These well-known verses call us to love our enemies. The use of hearts of all shapes and sizes could be arranged with a more prominent heart placed in the center that is "opened" by a fold.

Eighth Sunday after the Epiphany

Isaiah 49:8-16a	Consider taking the words "Engraved on the palms of God's hands" literally and make a big outline of a hand on a board. In the middle draw a heart on the palm like a tattoo.
Psalm 131 or Psalm 62:5-12	One very large rock placed on your display table will open thoughts of God as our rock and salvation.

| 1 Corinthians 4:1-5 | "Respect, Judge Not, Accept, Listen" . . . these words can be written on signs or boards. Or pick the verse from this reading that will be emphasized in the message and do the same. |
| Matthew 6:24-34 | This reading tells us to trust in God, using birds and the lilies of the field as examples. Make a bouquet of lilies and place them on your display. You may use artificial lilies. You will find origami directions at http://www.origami-instructions.com/origami-lily.html or have children make lilies using the directions at this web site: http://www.ehow.com/how_6509842_make-paper-easter-lilies.html. |

Ninth/Last Sunday after Epiphany/ Transfiguration Sunday

Exodus 24:12-18	All the readings today refer to moments of transformation and light. Finding prints from curriculum pieces and displaying them work well. In this reading, Moses on the mount is the theme. You could also use an item referring to the Ten Commandments.
Psalm 99	Exalt the holiness of God with visions of light using creative ways to symbolize the aura of God. A sunrise picture might work here.
2 Peter 1:16-21 and Matthew 17:1-9	As in the description above, use symbols to represent Jesus' glow at the transfiguration.

YEAR A

LENT

L ent is a forty-day period (excluding Sundays) prior to Easter. Forty is a popular number in the Bible, indicating the time necessary to fulfill what is to be done. The color for Lent is purple, representing royalty and our penitence. As we prepare to meet our King, we recognize our unworthiness and know that we must repent. Ash Wednesday signals the start of the season of Lent, this time of our asking forgiveness for our wrong ways.

Ash Wednesday

The Scriptures for this day are the same for all three years. All suggestions are placed in Year A. Ash Wednesday heralds the season of Lent, this time of our asking forgiveness for our wrong ways.

Joel 2:1-2, 12-17   A U-Turn sign or a model of a merry-go-round could represent, in a modern way, the theme of repentance, returning, and turning around. You might add a cross over the U-turn symbol. Or a heart might be added, since the reading suggests we rent our hearts and return to God.

Psalm 51:1-17

A simple tunic made from white sackcloth-type material, marred with soot from ash can be draped from your display. On another year, you might also consider adding a basin and soap bar on top of the white sackcloth-type material, marred with soot.

Consider using a large fireproof bowl and give the worshipers a piece of paper to write some sin they wish to have forgiven. Some time during the service have them place the papers in the bowl. Then during the service take the bowl outside and burn the papers and place the bowl with ashes on the table. These ashes will be too hot to use for marking the foreheads, so prepare ashes ahead of time for this. You might save this year's ashes for use next year. Some churches burn the palm fronds from the previous year, or burn some of the Christmas evergreens.

2 Corinthians 5:20b–6:10

Jesus' character of servanthood is always beautifully displayed with the use of a basin and towel. Another way to recognize our work for God is to place on a draped table symbols of the various ministries and missions your church regularly participates in.

Matthew 6:1-6, 16-21	A display of a treasure chest works very well for this reading.
	If you use this Scripture to emphasize the Lord's Prayer, use a picture or sculpting of praying hands. The picture of praying hands by Albrecht Dürer is appropriate here because of the humble nature it portrays. For the story behind the painting, go to: http://www.barefootsworld.net/albrechtdurer.html.

First Sunday in Lent

Genesis 2:15-17; 3:1-7	An old representation of the temptation in Genesis could be a bowl of apples with one set out on the side. (There is no reference to the fruit being an apple in the Bible, but this symbol has become popular.)
Psalm 32	God helps us be upright in our hearts. This psalm blesses us and can be symbolized with hearts.
Romans 5:12-19	A cross perfectly represents the concept of justification by the death of Jesus for us.
Matthew 4:1-11	The temptation of Jesus is not an easy idea to represent. Perhaps the simple words from verse 10, "Worship the Lord your God, and serve him only" works well.

Second Sunday in Lent

Genesis 12:1-4a   Remember making an old-fashioned string of paper dolls attached hand to hand when you were young? Make a few of these and place them on a display to represent the many that we are called to bless because we were first blessed.

Psalm 121   A shepherd is a wonderful symbol of God the keeper and protector of us all. The display could be a single shepherd, or one with a flock of sheep.

Romans 4:1-5, 13-17   Being justified by faith is a gift we can only thank God for in a deep-felt prayer of thanksgiving. A simple drawing or model of praying hands is an open-ended hint of grace.

John 3:1-17   There are many portraits and images of Jesus. Pick your favorite and display on an easel. Be sure that the image of Jesus reflects his ethnic Middle East background.

Third Sunday in Lent

Exodus 17:1-7   If you can run electricity to your display site, use a fountain made of rocks. You may find that someone has a fountain that you can borrow. Or, make a display of rocks sitting in water. Another suggestion is a large, clear pitcher of water.

Psalm 95   Sheep, a shepherd, or a shepherd's crook makes a good display here.

Romans 5:1-11   A nice, tall, glass pitcher of water with a glass cup next to it symbolizes a quenched thirst.

| John 4:5-42 | You might be able to find a small-sized pump to display. Or construct an old-style well easily built with large cardboard blocks and a bucket on a rope on its wall. A youth class may enjoy making such a well from Lego blocks. |

Fourth Sunday in Lent

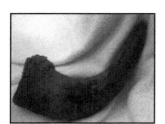

1 Samuel 16:1-13	Display a ram's horn vessel that holds oil or perhaps a modern vessel of anointing oil.
Psalm 23	Like last week, consider symbols of a shepherd, sheep, or shepherd's crook for your display.
Ephesians 5:8-14 and John 9:1-41	Both New Testament readings call for us to awake and see the light. A lit light bulb, if you have a source of electricity, is a modern symbol of both light and having our eyes opened.

Fifth Sunday in Lent

Ezekiel 37:1-14	From a science lab or high school/college professor you might be able to borrow a skeleton to put on display. It may be shocking, but it is effective.
Psalm 130 and Romans 8:6-11	To symbolize a cry of hope and for a spirit greater than mere mortality, a banner with drawing of arms and hands raised high done in a creative fashion will work.
John 11:1-45	Create a display of bands of cloth and simple bandages to remind people of the story of Lazarus being raised.

Sixth Sunday in Lent (Passion/Palm Sunday)

Some of the Scriptures for this day are the same as for other years. Check the other years for suggestions.

Liturgy of the Palms

Psalm 118:1-2, 19-29 and Matthew 21:1-11 — A banner with the words, "Blessed is he who comes in the name of the Lord" and "Hosanna" on it can be displayed in a variety of ways.

Liturgy of the Passion

Isaiah 50:4-9a — Use any symbol of a teacher, either modern, such as a ruler and an apple, or a print of a rabbi from Jesus' time for this display.

Psalm 31:9-16 — A large cracked or broken jar works perfectly for this Scripture.

Philippians 2:5-11 — Your worship space will undoubtedly be adorned with palms. You can always add more in an arrangement on your table.

Matthew 26:14–27:66 or 27:11-54 — Create a simple display of a cup, plate, bread, and grapes.

Monday of Holy Week

The Scriptures for this day are the same for all three years. All suggestions are placed in Year A.

Isaiah 42:1-9 — All new things will spring forth is simply and beautifully symbolized with a pot and a single sprout of new growth coming from it.

Psalm 36:5-11	Set up a running fountain to depict the fountain of life.
Hebrews 9:11-15	Christ's sacrifice is symbolized by a cross. One or several can be arranged.
John 12:1-11	As on the fifth Sunday of Lent, the use of strips of cloth and bandages works well.

Tuesday of Holy Week

The Scriptures for this day are the same for all three years. All suggestions are placed in Year A.

Isaiah 49:1-7	The theme for this reading includes Israel, the chosen people, servant, and called. Look for a variety of prints in past curriculum materials. Consider displaying a picture of the masses of Hebrew people.
Psalm 71:1-14	Find a shield of armor to display to represent God's protection.
1 Corinthians 1:18-31	To symbolize the "foolishness" of God, wiser than men, use the masks often found representing the theater . . . one smiling and one with a frown.
John 12:20-36	Using multiple tiny tea lights makes a nice display, representing children of the light.

Wednesday of Holy Week

The Scriptures for this day are the same for all three years. All suggestions are placed in Year A.

Isaiah 50:4-9a	Again, use symbols of a teacher such as a ruler and an apple.
Psalm 70	Use calligraphy to write the words, "Come, God, my help and deliverer" on a wide ribbon and display it for all to see.
Hebrews 12:1-3	Bring in a pair of running shoes and display them with a bottle of water.
John 13:21-32	A simple coin bag with silver coins thrown around the bag will represent the story of the betrayal by Judas.

Holy Thursday

The Scriptures for this day are the same for all three years. All suggestions are placed in Year A.

Exodus 12:1-4 (5-10) 11-14	Create a display with a large wooden staff as the focus to signify the staff of Moses. Not a shepherd's crook, but a staff works well.
Psalm 116:1-4, 12-19	As mentioned before, displaying musical instruments or symbols of music are perfect for any of the Psalm readings.
1 Corinthians 11:23-26	Nothing symbolizes Maundy Thursday better than the simple elements of the Eucharist. A cup, plate, bread, and grapes help us remember.

John 13:1-17, 31b-35 — And like the cup and bread for the Eucharist, a display of a bowl, pitcher, and towel reminds us of Jesus' great example of servanthood expressed in his act of foot washing.

Good Friday

The Scriptures for this day are the same for all three years. All suggestions are placed in Year A. No color or a black drape on the cross.

Isaiah 52:13–53:12 — A collection of sheep figurines, stuffed animals, or sheep made by the children of the church symbolizes the familiar phrase from Isaiah, "We all, like sheep."

Psalm 22 — Jesus quoted the first verse from this psalm at his crucifixion, "Why have you forsaken me?" Since our hearts are centered on the cross this day, a simple wooden cross and a handful of very large nails makes an effective display. And since this quotation was a question, and one we may ask ourselves, a display of question marks works well too.

Hebrews 10:16-25 — The life of Jesus was and is a gift of love. Display a heart.

John 18:1–19:42 — We remember the story of betrayal and of Peter's betrayal by the crowing of the cock. Consider placing a rooster figure on display.

Holy Saturday/Easter Vigil

The Scriptures for this day are the same for all three years. All suggestions are placed in Year A. The colors for today are white and/or gold.

Job 14:1-14	What a wonderful transition toward Easter to meditate on the thought from death to life. Take a walk outside or go to a nursery to find a bare branch with a single green shoot growing from it. You may also make this by taking a branch from a house plant and stripping all the leaves except one shoot.
Psalm 31:1-4, 15-16	To represent the concept of God as the rock of salvation, use a very large rock on your display.
1 Peter 4:1-8	Have the palms of hands dipped in paint and then stamped on a large banner. The hands symbolize helping hands and acts of charity. Or you may ask the children's teachers to outline each child's hands on construction paper, cut them out, and place them on the table.
Matthew 27:57-66	Construct a tomb with a stone securely at the entrance or post a print of the sealed tomb for this day. A youth class may like to make this tomb construction.

EASTER

Easter lasts from Easter Sunday until Pentecost. Too often we rejoice on Easter and fail to realize that the whole season is one of joy and celebration! We use white as a color for Easter.

Easter Sunday

The Scriptures for this day are the same for all three years. All suggestions are placed in Year A. Today the color is white and/or gold. More than any other day of the year, bring out your most festive, celebratory symbols and creativity.

Acts 10:34-43	For a symbol of "Christ for ALL" use a globe.
Psalm 118:1-2, 14-24	Consider a section of a fence opened with colorful, blooming flowers all around. Let it be extravagant in its mention of life.
Colossians 3:1-4	Put together symbols of love and affection using hearts, roses, or balloons with streamers and confetti for a beautiful display.

John 20:1-18 or
Matthew 28:1-10

A living display of butterflies is an amazing display. Live butterflies can be ordered (www. livebug.com) and displayed in what is called butterfly pavilion. In with the butterflies, add twigs with blooming buds. The beautiful movement of the butterflies reminds us of new life.

Second Sunday of Easter

Acts 2:14a, 22-32

Since the first reading this week tells of David's prophecy of the Christ, consider using symbols, figures, or an artistic print of a crowd of people to represent the many witnesses that have heard the Word.

Psalm 16

Signs of comfort work well for this reading about the presence of God. One example would be a collection of prayer shawls, lap robes, or a cozy quilt.

1 Peter 1:3-9

Our faith is more precious than gold. Create a display with a treasure chest adorned with gold colored jewels and coins. Or use a box with gold colored necklaces and coins spilling out.

John 20:19-31

The theme of John's Scripture is peace. The use of peace signs or the hanging of origami peace cranes would be nice. Go to http://www.origami-fun.com/origami-crane.html for directions.

Third Sunday of Easter

Acts 2:14a, 36-41	Water, doves, or other symbols of baptism will tie the worshipers' thoughts to the story of the baptism of the three thousand. See page 37 for instructions to make doves.
Psalm 116:1-4, 12-19	A banner with "Praise the Lord!" printed on it, or on a ribbon cascading around a trumpet or some other musical instrument works well here.
1 Peter 1:17-23	Consider printing the words "Hope" and "Faith" on signs and placing them on floral picks, displayed in a rich, green plant.
Luke 24:13-35	This well-known story of the risen Christ being revealed on the road to Emmaus and later breaking the bread brings to mind the sustaining symbols of the loaf. Take several loaves of bread in different styles and shapes. Place them in a big basket lined with a cloth. Take one of the loaves and break it in two, placing it to the side.

Fourth Sunday of Easter

Acts 2:42-47	A perfect symbol of this Scripture is anything representing abundance. We suggest using a basket overflowing with fruit and/or vegetables for this display area. Citrus fruits or a variety of apples make a gorgeous sight.
Psalm 23 and 1 Peter 2:19-25	A shepherd, sheep, a shepherd's crook . . . all will make perfect props to use for this most famous psalm and for the shepherd reference in 1 Peter.

John 10:1-10 Again, this reading has reference to the sheep. Along with the props used above, you can add a section of a gate as the backdrop.

Fifth Sunday of Easter

Acts 7:55-60 The killing of Stephen by stoning is a hard story of martyrdom. Use a small grouping of fist-size stones here.

Psalm 31:1-5, 15-16 Symbolize God as our refuge and rock with a large rock.

1 Peter 2:2-10 Both the Psalter and the 1 Peter reading call forth visions of committing our spirits to God. We have been called to be chosen people of the light. Take many, many tea lights and display them on a beautiful cloth to represent our many spirits.

John 14:1-14 Take a large mirror and prop it up on your display. Either write on a long ribbon, or write on the mirror with a washable marker or washable paint, the words, "I am in the Father, and the Father is in me." If you use the ribbon, drape it across the mirror.

Sixth Sunday of Easter

The theme of this Sunday is God creator of all; alive in the spirit around us.

Acts 17:22-31	In this reading we hear of God, creator of all and alive in the spirit around us. These words in verse 28, "In Him we live and move and have our being," gives the heart of the message. Take a large piece of paper and use many words representing spirit written in various sizes, colors, and styles.
Psalm 66:8-20	This psalm reminds us of Saint Francis of Assisi. There are many garden statues of this famous follower. Use one to represent him.
1 Peter 3:13-22	The vignette can be full of symbols of different professions to remind us to use our own gifts to do good works.
John 14:15-21	You can best symbolize the concept of the spirit of truth by asking the preacher what truths might be lifted up in the service this day. For example, if the lesson is for us to speak out for others that are disenfranchised, a megaphone and a soapbox could serve well. It is good to be in dialogue with the one preaching.

Ascension Sunday

Acts 1:1-11	If you have a power source, set up small spotlights aimed toward the ceiling at different angles for a dramatic display. You can even use different-colored bulbs for an interesting effect.

Psalm 47	Sing praises with a display of musical symbols as has been mentioned before. Most all Psalter readings have a strong tie to musical representation since most psalms are songs.
Ephesians 1:15-23	This reading speaks of the church as the body of Christ. If your church has a pictorial directory, display it for this reading. Or you could use a display of several snapshots of your congregation working and worshiping in your community.
Luke 24:44-53	Focus either on the empty tomb or the ascension of the post-crucified Jesus by using prints of Christian art. Old curriculum pieces offer many opportunities here. Check your church library for illustrations as well and display the open book.

Seventh Sunday of Easter

Acts 1:6-14	A circle of friends or a small grouping of people reminds us of those in attendance in the upper room. One suggestion is to use a photo or drawing of a group of people with a candle in the middle.
Psalm 68:1-10, 32-35	You can easily represent God's character as protector by taking an umbrella, opening it up, and placing it on your display table.
1 Peter 4:12-14; 5:6-11	Consider using hands in prayer, prayer beads, or a prayer book to remind us to hold our faith close in times of anxiety.
John 17:1-11	Symbolize unity and oneness with an old-fashioned string of people cut from folded paper. Place them in a circle, connecting all of the "hands."

PENTECOST

Sometimes we call Pentecost the birthday of the church. This was a celebration that Jesus' followers observed, and when they were together they received the Holy Spirit. Too often we fail to recognize this important date in our calendar. We use red for Pentecost to represent the flames that came on the disciples' heads as they gathered on the Jewish holy day of Pentecost. Some churches will use red for several Sundays after Pentecost and then change to green. Some change to green after Trinity Sunday. Here green represents the spread of Christ's word throughout the world.

Day of Pentecost

Acts 2:1-21	We have many voices in our diversity, yet we are all one. Find a poster of the different symbols of the denominations or faith communities to display. Also check with years B and C because the same Scripture is used there.
Psalm 104:24-34, 35b	Open a large Bible to this week's Psalter reading and place it on your display table. Then surround the Bible with different figurines of people, animals, and flowers—for God is the creator of ALL.

| 1 Corinthians 12:3b-13 | To depict the variety of gifts, consider props representing different professions. Use a cooking pot, hammer, stethoscope, book, ruler, and the like. |
| John 7:37-39 | Use a flowing, tabletop fountain if you have a power source. If not, place a large pitcher of water and a cup to make a meaningful display. |

Trinity Sunday or First Sunday after Pentecost

Genesis 1:1–2:4a and Psalm 8	We pause to reflect on the beauty of God's creation. Hang a mobile of our solar system and let the air currents move the planets during the service as the congregation meditates.
2 Corinthians 13:11-13	Our God is one of love and peace. Use your favorite symbols of these words to make a display. Since it is Trinity Sunday, use a grouping of three to add the dimension of trinity.
Matthew 28:16-20	Find a pair of old worn work boots and put them on display. To be sent out to make disciples requires work and connecting. The boots will signify this action.

YEAR A

ORDINARY TIME (AFTER PENTECOST)

G reen is the color of this season. Using the word "ordinary" does not mean mundane or common. It comes from the word *ordinal,* which means simply counted or chronological time. In this case, it refers to the weeks as they follow one another in order.

Second Sunday after Pentecost

Genesis 22:1-14	Take several smooth stones of a variety of sizes and stack them one on top of the other. This beautiful symbol is used worldwide and represents an altar.
Psalm 13	This psalm is about trusting God. Use the words from Proverbs 3:5 to create a word display of trust, "Trust in the LORD with all your heart."
Romans 6:12-23	This reading offers another opportunity to use a single word or phrase to connect to idea of presenting ourselves to God. Display the word "Confession" in a variety of ways. We come to God confessing, asking forgiveness, and trusting in God's grace.

Matthew 10:40-42 — As we have suggested before, a clear pitcher and cup of cold water are perfect props for this reading. Or consider a hand pump.

Third Sunday after Pentecost

Genesis 24:34-38, 42-49, 58-67 — When a scripture reading tells a story directly, consider using a symbol of that story. In this case, an old water jar simply placed on display reminds us of Rebecca, Isaac, and Abraham.

Psalm 45:10-17 or Psalm 72 — Make a form in the shape of a tree and add leaves with names on them—a family tree. This symbol reminds us of our ancestry.

Romans 7:15-25a — As humans, we all struggle with will and sin and right choices. To symbolize this struggle, create a diorama of a wall with multiple doors. Label each as door 1, door 2, and door 3.

Matthew 11:16-19, 25-30 — A yoke makes an appropriate symbol for this reading.

Fourth Sunday after Pentecost

Genesis 25:19-34 — During this season, the Old Testament readings follow stories of our Hebrew ancestors. Prints from illustrated books or old curriculum materials displayed can give a symbol of each story. This week, two blue baby blankets could symbolize the boy twins, Jacob and Esau.

Psalm 119:105-12 or Psalm 25 Romans 8:1-11

Paint a series of curved lines on a large banner of opaque netting to represent the wind. Hang or drape this to represent the Spirit. To represent a lamp and light to guide us, place a collection of lights or lamps together.

Matthew 13:1-9, 18-23

Pour a pile of rich soil on your table and add some pots and seed packets to illustrate the parable of the soils.

Fifth Sunday after Pentecost

Genesis 28:10-19a

What better prop than a ladder for the story of Jacob's dream. Use one that opens in an inverted V to stand up. They come in a variety of heights to keep in scale with your space.

Psalm 139:1-12, 23-24 and Romans 8:12-25

A tasteful image or figurine of a full-term, pregnant woman would represent both the womb and labor of creation for these two readings.

Matthew 13:24-30, 36-43

The use of weeds and wheat works wonders for this Scripture. Be sure to have an obvious difference in the two cuttings so there is no doubt that one is a weed and one is a healthy harvest. Place them side by side in the display.

Sixth Sunday after Pentecost

Genesis 29:15-28	Construct a Jewish *chuppah* to signify a wedding canopy. It is a modern symbol of a Jewish marriage. Make it with a large square of fabric attached to four poles. See http://www.ehow.com/how_2322134_make-secular-chuppah.html#ixzz1NNc2ZZiP. Jacob married, over time, the two sisters Leah and Rachel.
Psalm 105:1-11, 45b	Place a large Torah, either in book form or scrolls, on display. The Hebrew text teaches us all about the works of God through history as explained by the people of faith.
Romans 8:26-39	Nothing can separate us from God's love. This message becomes personal by making a very large heart and placing a photo of your congregation in the middle of it.
Matthew 13:31-33, 44-52	Many times Jesus talked about what heaven and how life itself "is like." Objects he used were treasures, pearls, mustard seeds, and yeast. You can use any or all of these. You can also take a large fishing net and drape it over your table with other fishing objects on it.

Seventh Sunday after Pentecost

Genesis 32:22-31	Display a large mirror or a standing mirror to remind us of Jacob seeing God "face to face."
Psalm 17:1-7, 15	Place a nice pair of walking shoes on display to remind others that we are to keep walking in righteousness.

Romans 9:1-5 — The heartfelt affection for the Jewish people that Paul wrote about as he made reference to his kindred Israelites is touching. Use a family tree or a painting of Israelites from history for this display.

Matthew 14:13-21 — There is nothing like our Bible to show where to turn when finding ways to live with inner righteousness. Place a large Bible on display open to these verses in Matthew. Place a small candle next to it to represent our inner light.

Eighth Sunday after Pentecost

Genesis 37:1-4, 12-28
Psalm 105:1-6, 16-22, 45b
Romans 10:5-15
Matthew 14:22-33 — All four readings focus on the virtues of faith, perseverance, and patience. A wonderful display of an old fishing boat represents the faith we place in God while we journey in our own lifeboats as well as the story of leaving the boat to walk on water in faith.

Ninth Sunday after Pentecost

Genesis 45:1-15 — Again, consider using a photo from past curriculum materials to show the story of Joseph reconciled to his brothers.

Psalm 133	To make a modern display sharing the message of living together in unity, go to an auto parts shop and ask to borrow a smaller size car bumper. Place a bumper sticker "Coexist" on the bumper. You can create your own bumper sticker on a rectangular-shaped piece of paper.	
Romans 11:1-2a, 29-32	A display made of hearts would represent well the forgiving mercy of God even after disobedience.	
Matthew 15:21-28	Find a shiny armor shield to display as a symbol of Jesus' salvation.	

Tenth Sunday after Pentecost

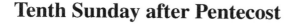

Exodus 1:8–2:10 and Psalm 124	The message of this psalm expresses how God delivers us. The Exodus story of Moses being saved from the river is an example of deliverance. Use a baby Moses in a basket with a blanket.
Romans 12:1-8	The theme of our diversity within our unity as we are one in Christ opens up a wide variety of illustrations and artistic possibilities. Consider using many different strips of fabrics woven together in a single piece.
Matthew 16:13-20	Simply write on a banner or wide ribbon the words "Who do you say I am?" to cause others to think.

Eleventh Sunday after Pentecost

Exodus 3:1-15	If you have a power source, you can take a mini-sized fan and place it under a small pile of logs. Attach two- to three-feet-long strips of orange, yellow, and red crepe paper. Turn on and watch the fan blow the paper like flames . . . flames that do not burn.
Psalm 105:1-6, 23-26, 45c	As in previous entries, the visual of a tree with leaves or a family tree chart can be displayed.
Romans 12:9-21	Take a long roll of paper and title it, "How to Live a Christian Life." Create a "checklist" of Christian living values that come to mind as you read this Scripture. Place the list next to a bucket. Display your "bucket list" for all to see.
Matthew 16:21-28	Reference to a cross is notable when actually using the cross.

Twelfth Sunday after Pentecost

Exodus 12:1-14	Collect and display all the symbols and pieces used in a Seder meal including the menorah and cup.
Psalm 149 or Psalm 148	We have used this before, but again it makes a perfect banner when the words "Gloria in Excelsis Deo" are done in calligraphy. Psalm 148 is also used in the first Sunday after Christmas for all three years. Check those suggestions.

Romans 13:8-14 | This important lesson, found in all the major religions, can be displayed with a collage of hearts.

Matthew 18:15-20 | To represent the gathering of two or three, take figurines or human figures and pose them together.

Thirteenth Sunday after Pentecost

Exodus 14:19-31 | A staff such as that of Moses or a diorama of the parting of the sea is a great visual for this story.

Exodus 15:1b-11, 20-21 | Musical symbols are often suggested for the Psalter reading. This week use tambourines and cymbals to represent Miriam's song and dance.

Romans 14:1-12 | To symbolize the message of not judging one another use a judge's gavel or measure weights.

Matthew 18:21-35 | When you display three crosses together, it reminds the viewer of Jesus forgiving the sinners hanging on the crosses next to him at his own crucifixion.

Fourteenth Sunday after Pentecost

Exodus 16:2-15 | To illustrate the story of manna, put together a grouping of grasses or low plants. Then pull small pieces of cotton balls, gauze, or white string and place it in the greenery. This is what the manna may have looked like each day it was given to the Hebrews.

Psalm 105:1-6, 37-45 or Psalm 78	What a wonderful symbol of storytelling comes from the Native American tradition. Consider using either a totem pole or a storytelling doll as your prop this week.
Philippians 1:21-30	Symbols of spirit such as the dove or wind can be used along with a phrase in the reading that coordinates with the message. See page 37 for instructions to make doves.
Matthew 20:1-16	The parable of the workers paid equally can be represented with a wagon wheel, as its parts are of equal size. If your space is small, you might use a simple pie cut equally into a few pieces and pulled slightly apart to show the division.

Fifteenth Sunday after Pentecost

Exodus 17:1-7	The Hebrews wanted their drink of water. A stick like the one Moses used as he traveled can be displayed. Or, perhaps, a vessel of water.
Psalm 78:1-4, 12-16	The importance of telling the story to children is beautifully depicted in the storyteller doll from the Native American tradition.
Philippians 2:1-13	Use the towel, basin, and pitcher as a reminder to serve each other as exemplified in Jesus' act of washing the feet of others.
Matthew 21:23-32	Don't just say what is right, do what's right. Use a banner of handprints and footprints to symbolize the doing.

Sixteenth Sunday after Pentecost

Exodus 20:1-4, 7-9, 12-20	Two tablets representing the Ten Commandments makes a perfect prop for this story.
Psalm 19	The words: "Law of the LORD is . . . perfect, sure, right, clear, pure, and true" make a nice sign that can be displayed here.
Philippians 3:4b-14	Print the letters J-O-Y on several helium balloons and attach them at a variety of heights at your display site.
Matthew 21:33-46	A big, overflowing basket of fruit makes a colorful representation of the reward to those who produce fruit.

Seventeenth Sunday after Pentecost

Exodus 32:1-14	If you can find a golden calf or a print of that story's scene, use it. Or make a display of many gold-colored pieces of jewelry, coins, and artifacts.
Psalm 106:1-6, 19-23	Using a visual of praying hands makes a good symbol for petition and the reference of Moses' interceding for the Hebrews.
Philippians 4:1-9	Write the word "Rejoice" in calligraphy and display. Decorate the banner or sign with glitter and streamers to make it as joyful as you can.
Matthew 22:1-14	Make a long list of first names, using as many names within your congregation as you can. This list will represent the guest list of those invited to the wedding.

Eighteenth Sunday after Pentecost

Exodus 33:12-23	Moses was aware of the presence of God, even though he did not see God's face. Moses turned away. You might put up a figure of a man wearing a blindfold. If you make your own drawing of this visual, add up-stretched arms.
Psalm 99	A scale of justice can depict God's justice and fairness in the Old Testament sense.
1 Thessalonians 1:1-10	One of the most beloved hymns and musical messages is that of "Great Is Thy Faithfulness." Take the sheet music, enlarge in a copier, and display on a tabletop easel or music stand.
Matthew 22:15-22	Take a simple coin purse and scatter coins around it.

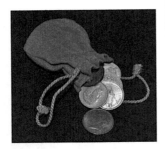

Nineteenth Sunday after Pentecost

Deuteronomy 34:1-12	Use a torch similar to the style used in the Olympics to represent being a witness and passing of the torch for this story.
Psalm 90:1-6, 13-17	Being with God, being at home with God, and going to God is often felt emotionally by people as they worship in their sanctuary. Display a photograph of your church or the worship place.
1 Thessalonians 2:1-8	Use a display of valentines to depict the love letter to the Thessalonians.
Matthew 22:34-46	Love God and love your neighbor. This message is all about love and the use of valentines can be used here as well hearts in general.

Twentieth Sunday after Pentecost

Joshua 3:7-17	Use a print from curriculum materials or an illustration marking the journey Joshua takes with the people over the Jordan River.
Psalm 107:1-7, 33-37	This song of God's deliverance can use symbols of music and song.
1 Thessalonians 2:9-13	There are many accessible figurines of a parent with a child or children that you may use here.
Matthew 23:1-12	Matthew portrays Jesus as a teacher of rightful living and lessons on relationship in this passage. Modern symbols of teaching such as rulers, books, and apples can be put together in a teaching display.

All Saints Day or Sunday

Red and white are the colors of All Saints Day.

Revelation 7:9-17	Use many signs of ALL the people gathered by combining the different symbols of denominations.
Psalm 34:1-10, 22	Call on God can be symbolized by placing an old-style telephone on the table.
1 John 3:1-3	If possible, collect a photo of each child in your congregation. If your congregation is large, take photos of each Sunday school class. Then on a poster board make a collage of all the children together.
Matthew 5:1-12	Find a very large candelabra or candle stick and light a bright candle to represent the call to let your light shine.

Twenty-first Sunday after Pentecost

Joshua 24:1-3a, 14-25	Like Joshua, we will serve God. Display the words, "As for me and my household, we will serve the LORD."
Psalm 78:1-7	In many places throughout Scripture, we are commanded to teach and tell the stories of faith to our children. Again, the storyteller doll is perfect.
1 Thessalonians 4:13-18	The symbol of a yoke can be used many times in displays. Being yoked to the eternal life with Christ is another opportunity to use a yoke in display.
Matthew 25:1-13	Be ready for God. We get ready each day at the sound of the alarm clock. We have used this prop before, and it works here as well.

Twenty-second Sunday after Pentecost

Judges 4:1-7	Deborah as a woman judge in ancient Israel is a nice visual, especially for girls and women of the church. Use old curriculum pictures or illustrations of Deborah, or simply use a judge's gavel.
Psalm 123 or Psalm 76	Open a large Bible and place a pair of eyeglasses on top. This symbol reminds us of the message to look to God.
1 Thessalonians 5:1-11	Light is the symbol of those waiting for Christ's return in this particular Scripture. Use candles of many sizes for your display. Or use children's simple drawings showing the rising sun.
Matthew 25:14-30	Use copies of made-up loan documents with a stack of dollars next to it to illustrate the parable of the loan.

Christ the King/Reign of Christ

The colors are white and gold.

Ezekiel 34:11-16, 20-24 and Psalm 100	Display a shepherd's crook.
Ephesians 1:15-23	Proudly display a photograph of your church building or a collage of church members doing the many ministries of your congregation.
Matthew 25:31-46	Any sign of servanthood such as the towel and basin or prints of the hands of many may be displayed.

Thanksgiving Day

The color for this day is red or green. Check the other years for additional Thanksgiving ideas.

Deuteronomy 8:7-18 Psalm 65 2 Corinthians 9:6-15 Luke 17:11-19	An abundant display of plenty is perfect for this day of thanks. Use a cornucopia, basket, or crate overflowing with fruits, vegetables, breads, and gifts.

YEAR B

ADVENT

See Year A (page 27) for information on Advent. The colors are purple or blue.

First Sunday of Advent

This Sunday not only presents a theme of watching and waiting, but the responsibility of each person to look for places that the presence of God is obvious, even in this time.

Isaiah 64:1-9	This Scripture speaks of God as the potter and us as the clay. For this, you might use a piece of pottery as the center visual, placing it on draped purple cloth.
Psalm 80:1-7, 17-19	The Psalter reading asks that God listen to us and give us guidance. A picture of a hand or a sculpted hand would give a good visual image for this reading.
1 Corinthians 1:3-9	The reading from the letters encourages us to look for places that God's presence is evident by recognizing the spiritual gifts we have been given. Use a collection of items that represent our gifts or talents, such as pen and paper, cooking utensil, musical instrument, artist's brush, sports equipment, and such.

Mark 13:24-37   You might choose from two images for this Gospel reading. The first is obvious, that of an angel. However, we'd suggest an image that relates to our physical world, that of a bare limb of a tree that has obvious buds on it that will open in the spring. This could then be referenced as the obvious promise of God that spring will come, just as God has promised the coming of the Son of Man.

Second Sunday of Advent

This Sunday announces the good tidings or good news of the coming of Christ who will herald a new time, a time of peace. With it will come the challenge to follow him in order to bring about that peace.

Isaiah 40:1-11   This familiar reading of Isaiah speaks of making straight the pathway of our Lord. A photo of a straight road in the desert would be appropriate here, or you might do something a little different by using a flat box or tray and placing sand in it. Create a pathway through the sand that begins as a curving path and then becomes straight, using small stones to line the pathway.

Psalm 85:1-2, 8-13   This reading from the Psalms is one of peace. We use the dove as a symbol of peace, and so a white dove nestled in the folds of a purple cloth would be appropriate here. You might also use the modern-day sign for peace. See page 37 for instructions for making doves.

2 Peter 3:8-15a	This famous passage about waiting can be illustrated in visual form by collecting many pages of a calendar. Tear out pages from the calendars and mass them on top of a drape of purple cloth, spilling them over from the table onto the floor. Indeed, God's time is not set in hours, months, or even years. God's time is eternal.
Mark 1:1-8	The Gospel reading for this Sunday stresses the preparation of a pathway for the Lord. The suggestion for the reading in Isaiah also lends itself to this passage.

Third Sunday of Advent

This Sunday we consider the deliverer, Christ, who will break from the old to create a new freedom for those who are bound in the chains of the past. This is a time of hope, a new day, a new beginning! Rejoice in it!

Isaiah 61:1-4, 8-11	This Scripture is rich with images as we anticipate the coming of the deliverer. The image that comes foremost to mind is that of a broken chain, symbolizing the release of the captives. Consider having someone walk slowly down the center aisle during the first hymn (perhaps "Hail to the Lord's Anointed") carrying a chain, and either placing it on the table or draping it across a cross. You might also use a garland of flowers over a heap of ashes. Verse 11 can be illustrated by planting some grass seed in a pot ahead of time so that you have new shoots of grass.

Psalm 126	This Scripture promises joy after sorrow, sheaves and fruit after tears. You might use sheaves of wheat, or a more common symbol would be a large basket of fruit, full and spilling over. The fruit of the promised joy.
1 Thessalonians 5:16-24	In this letter, Paul encourages the Thessalonians to pray without ceasing. When using this as the main Scripture, consider using a large clock as a visual.
John 1:6-8, 19-28	This Scripture tells of John the Baptist's announcement of the Christ. Dramatically feature this Scripture with a drape of burlap cloth, first in folds on the left of the table, and then draped to a higher position on the right of the table. On top of the higher position, place a large lit candle. The burlap represents John the Baptist and leads to the candle, representing Christ.

Fourth Sunday of Advent

In this Sunday's readings, we see the promise of the Messiah, not only important to the Hebrews but also including the Gentiles. God's promise is for all!

2 Samuel 7:1-11, 16	David is promised a lineage, which we see leading to Jesus. As a visual, consider using a small tree as a "Jesse Tree," representing the ancestry of Jesus. Or you may even use an old root, representing David as the ancestor of Jesus.

Psalm 89:1-4, 19-26	Verse 19 speaks of the crown set on the one who is to be lifted up. If you use the image of a crown, place it high with a purple drape flowing from the crown down onto the table. You might place straw on the table below, symbolizing the birthplace of Christ. In verse 26 the psalmist speaks of the rock of our salvation. If you use the rock image, make it a large and solid rock.
Romans 16:25-27	Here Paul references the prophetic writings that made Christ known, even to the Gentiles. We would suggest that you use a Bible, open to one of the books of the prophets, and in front of the Bible place a picture of Jesus. Be sure that Jesus' features indicate his ethnic background. If you do not have an ethnic picture of Jesus, you may use a candle to represent Christ.
Luke 1:26-38	This is the announcement to Mary that she will deliver Christ to the world. This can be portrayed by using fabric. A blue drape would represent Mary, and a white drape would represent Jesus. Drape the blue fabric across the table and up on a higher position. Then place the white fabric within the blue, but coming out of the folds and spilling down the front.

Christmas Eve

The Scriptures for this day are the same for all three years. All suggestions are placed in Year A.

YEAR B

CHRISTMAS

See Year A (page 32) for information about the Christmas season. The colors of white, yellow, and gold may be used.

Christmas Sunday/Christmas Day

The Scriptures for this day are the same for all three years. All suggestions are placed in Year A.

First Sunday after Christmas

Isaiah 61:10–62:3	This Scripture speaks of the clothing of the righteous, and garlands and crowns. Against a white drape, you might place a gold drape and add a garland of bright artificial flowers or a crown.
Psalm 148	This psalm of praise can be visualized by placing replicas of the sun and stars on the draped table. Place the sun on the white, and place a dark blue drape over the part of the table on which you place stars of various sizes. Use varying heights for the stars. This Scripture is used for the first Sunday after Christmas in years A and C also. Check those suggestions.

Galatians 4:4-7 — This speaks of the coming of Christ as a gift to all people, Gentiles as well as Jews. This might be illustrated with a visual using small figures with features of various ethnic backgrounds, showing inclusiveness. Or you might use a globe or a large picture that simply shows a mass of people.

Luke 2:22-40 — This Scripture includes the Temple blessing of Jesus, which was a part of their custom for babies. In our churches we either baptize a baby, indicating the acceptance of that child into the family of God, or we have some sort of dedication if the church only observes believer baptism. If you use a rosebud to celebrate the birth of a baby, place a rosebud in a vase with the white drape beneath and behind it. Or use some modern-day baby items.

Watch Night/New Year's Eve/New Year's Day

The Scriptures for this day are the same for all three years. All suggestions are placed in Year A.

Second Sunday after Christmas

Jeremiah 31:7-14 — This gathering Scripture can be illustrated with either a globe or a large map of the world. If you use a map, place large arrows on the map, all pointing to Israel.

Psalm 147:12-20 — This song of praise might have a horn or even a tambourine to indicate our praise to God. Use any instrument that is typical of your individual church's way of praising God.

Ephesians 1:3-14 — The Ephesians passage speaks of the "seal of God" being placed on us, indicating the inclusiveness of our approval as a part of God's people, even if we are Gentiles. A large golden seal would be appropriate for this. Make it using gold foil over a large round of cardboard.

John 1:1-18 — For the reference here of the law being given through Moses and grace and truth through Christ, you might put a replica of the stones of the Ten Commandments on the table and place a cross over the Ten Commandments to represent Christ.

YEAR B

EPIPHANY

See Year A (page 36) for information on Epiphany. The color for Epiphany begins with white and then turns to green.

Epiphany Sunday

The Scriptures for this day are the same for all three years. All suggestions are placed in Year A.

Baptism of the Lord/First Sunday after the Epiphany

Genesis 1:1-5	This Scripture centers on creation, speaking specifically of the separation of light from darkness. Use a white and a black drape, placing them side by side. Be sure to elevate part of the drapes, allowing them to flow down onto the table. Symbolically, this also speaks of Christ bringing light into the world.
Psalm 29	In this psalm, David speaks of God's power and majesty, but he ends with a statement of God bringing peace. A picture of a lightning storm with a dove beside it might be appropriate here. See page 37 for instructions on making a dove.

Acts 19:1-7

Luke tells us, in this Scripture, that we must receive the Holy Spirit. The flame, a symbol of the Holy Spirit, may be used with this.

Mark 1:4-11

Use a dove with this Scripture of the baptism of Jesus. According to Mark, the dove came down from heaven. See page 37 for instructions on making a dove.

YEAR B

ORDINARY TIME (AFTER EPIPHANY)

See Year A (page 38) for information on Ordinary Time. We use green during this season.

Second Sunday after the Epiphany

1 Samuel 3:1-20	Samuel and Eli were in the temple of the Lord. We also consider our bodies as temples of the Lord, and we are each called, no matter our age. Considering this, pictures of people at all ages of life would be appropriate for this setting. Include a picture of an elementary child, a youth, and several stages of adulthood.
Psalm 139:1-6, 13-18	This passage speaks of God knowing us from the beginning, even as we were "knit" together in our mother's womb. Although a picture of a fetus comes to mind here, perhaps a picture of a newborn baby is more appropriate for our intergenerational worship.
1 Corinthians 6:12-20	This may be a hard Scripture to depict visually, but a picture of a healthy person can be used. Or you might place several items that we use to keep our bodies healthy, such as soap, toothbrush, and healthy food.

John 1:43-51	This is the calling of the disciples. If you have a picture of Jesus with his hand extended, as if asking us to follow, you can use it. Another possibility is placing a cross on one side of the table and then twelve stones on the other side of the table, indicating that Jesus called his twelve disciples to be the foundation of the church.

Third Sunday after the Epiphany

Jonah 3:1-5, 10	The passage skips the "big fish" part of the Jonah story and goes right to the theme of the season after Epiphany, to witness and spread the news to other peoples to change their ways and turn to God. Group together symbols of various ways that we can spread this message, including cell phones, letters, computers, and such.
Psalm 62:5-12	This is an appropriate passage for the use of a rock, since it speaks of God as the rock of our salvation.
1 Corinthians 7:29-31	Paul's letter here also deals with witnessing and telling others to turn from their old ways and acknowledge God. You may use the suggestion for the Jonah passage.
Mark 1:14-20	Since this passage deals with Jesus calling the disciples from their fishing careers, you may want to use a fishing net over the green drape. Bring it from a higher position and let it nestle on the table, then draping down over the front and onto the floor. The simplicity of this setting will speak of the simple lives of those whom Jesus called in this passage.

Fourth Sunday after the Epiphany

Deuteronomy 18:15-20	We often think of prophets as those who shouted condemnation, but actually the prophet was one who brought hope. For this passage, with the promise of a prophet, you may use the word "Hope" in some way, either with large cut-out letters or using calligraphy on a sign or on a banner.
Psalm 111	For this hymn of praise use bright colors to indicate the joy that comes with praising God. For this you might use coils of ribbon or a nest of colorful scarves.
1 Corinthians 8:1-13	This Scripture speaks of the stumbling blocks that we sometimes put before others with our examples. For this visual, find a flat stone, one that would not be obvious to a person walking casually down the street but that might be a stumbling block.
Mark 1:21-28	In this passage the spirits respected the authority of Jesus, and the people recognized that authority. This might be symbolized by placing a candle, representing Christ, over a dark drape that is nested on the table.

Fifth Sunday after the Epiphany

Isaiah 40:21-31	The end of this passage is very familiar. Those who rely on God mount up with wings like eagles. A picture of an eagle in flight would be an appropriate visual for this passage.

Psalm 147:1-11, 20c

1 Corinthians 9:16-23

Mark 1:29-39

Actually, all of the passages for this Sunday speak of God's power to heal and restore life. Any visuals that pertain to healing would be appropriate here.

Sixth Sunday after the Epiphany

2 Kings 5:1-14

This passage not only speaks of healing, but also of the arrogance that we sometimes have when we seek help. The commander of the army expected his healing to be spectacular. This theme may be portrayed with a sign with a red circle and line through it, using the word "Pride" in the crossed-out circle.

Psalm 30

This psalm speaks of the Lord taking off the sackcloth and replacing it with joy. Here you might use a dark fabric (or burlap bag). Position it at some height, then place colored ribbons or scarves so that they "spill" out of the dark fabric (or burlap bag).

1 Corinthians 9:24-27

For this Scripture, use several running shoes, some large and some small.

Mark 1:40-45

This story is more than a simple healing by Jesus. The leper is so overpowered by joy that he cannot keep quiet! The visual suggestion for Psalm 30 above may be used here as well.

Transfiguration Sunday/Last Sunday after the Epiphany

2 Kings 2:1-12
Psalm 50:1-6
2 Corinthians 4:3-6
Mark 9:2-9

All of these Scriptures speak of transfiguration and the brightness of the presence of God. Any visual that depicts brightness would be appropriate here. This might be a large candle, or you might use a large golden plate and shine a bright light on it. Using a drape of dark green as the background will make the bright object stand out more.

YEAR B

LENT

See Year A (page 44) for information on the season of Lent. We use purple for this season.

Ash Wednesday

The Scriptures for this day are the same for all three years. All suggestions are placed in Year A.

First Sunday in Lent

Genesis 9:8-17   For this story of Noah and God's covenant you may use a painting or figure of the ark. If that isn't available, place plastic animals on the focal center.

Psalm 25:1-10   This Scripture asks God to teach us direction or the paths we should follow. A picture of a path leading through the woods may be used, or you may create a path through a tray of sand, as suggested for Isaiah 40:1-11 in the second Sunday of Advent for this year.

1 Peter 3:18-22	If you use this Scripture to draw out the importance of our baptism, use a basin and pitcher, and at some time during the service, pour water from the pitcher into the basin. These might be brought down the aisle at the beginning of the service and placed on the draped table, perhaps during the first hymn.
Mark 1:9-15	The baptism font or basin can be displayed here, or you may use the suggestion for 1 Peter 3:18-22 above.

Second Sunday in Lent

Genesis 17:1-7, 15-16	The theme of this Scripture includes a promise from God, but along with the promise comes the responsibility. The change of names accompanies this responsibility. Make signs that say: Abram = Abraham and Sarai = Sarah. Or you may use the visual suggested below.
Psalm 22:23-31 Romans 4:13-25	For both Scriptures, a picture of masses of people or a globe portrays the theme that God rules over the whole world with inclusiveness, no matter what our physical heritage.
Mark 8:31-38	A cross is appropriate for this Scripture, but do not use it upright. Instead lay it down, propped so that it can be seen from the congregation. This helps us remember that we must take up the cross ourselves.

Third Sunday in Lent

Exodus 20:1-17	The usual display of the law of the Ten Commandments is on stone. However, to bring it to the modern congregation, print the commandments in a large font on parchment-type paper and place it on the draped table.
Psalm 19	To emphasize the "sweetness" of following God's law expressed in this Scripture, use the Ten Commandments with a jar of honey.
1 Corinthians 1:18-25	The cross may be used with this Scripture since it speaks of the "message of the cross."
John 2:13-22	This story of Jesus cleansing the Temple can be portrayed with a stack of coins and a large black X propped against the coins. Make the X from a black tagboard.

Fourth Sunday in Lent

Numbers 21:4-9 Psalm 107:1-3, 17-22	Using calligraphy or such a type font on the computer, create several signs with the word "Holy," symbolizing the importance of our seeing God as the one holy God.
Ephesians 2:1-10	Using calligraphy or such font on the computer, make one large sign with the word "Grace."
John 3:14-21	This passage includes John 3:16, which speaks of God's love. Since the heart is a popular symbol for love, you may use this as a focal point. However, at the close of this Scripture, John speaks of those who do what is true coming to the light. For emphasis on this section of the Scripture we'd suggest that you use a large candle, or some other source of light.

Fifth Sunday in Lent

Jeremiah 31:31-34	In this reading, Jeremiah tells of God making a new covenant with the people, writing it on their hearts. We believe that Christ brought about that new covenant, and so a picture of Christ (or the word "Christ") on a large heart would symbolize this understanding.
Psalm 51:1-12	As this psalm speaks of God washing us from our sins, a basin of water, towel, and soap would be a good visual. You might also include a small branch of hyssop if that is available. Hyssop is of the mint family, so you might substitute a spring of mint for this herb. However, we'd suggest that you explain, either orally or in a bulletin the substitution.
Hebrews 5:5-10	The reading from the Epistles claims Jesus as high priest. For a modern-day symbol of this use a plain cross and drape a liturgical stole over it.
John 12:20-33	There are several images you might use here. The suggestion above for Hebrews could be used, lifting up Christ. You might also use a sheaf of wheat, or even a bowl of wheat seed, emphasizing verse 24. Verse 26 speaks of serving as we follow Christ. For this choose a visual of service.

Sixth Sunday in Lent (Passion/Palm Sunday)

Liturgy of the Palms

The Scriptures for Liturgy of the Palms are the same for all three years. All suggestions are placed in Year A.

Liturgy of the Passion

Isaiah 50:4-9a
Psalm 31:9-16
Philippians 2:5-11
Matthew 26:14–
27:66 or 27:11-54

These Scriptures are the same for all three years. All suggestions are placed in Year A.

Monday through Saturday of Holy Week

The Scriptures for these days are the same for all three years. All suggestions are placed in Year A.

YEAR B

EASTER

See Year A (page 54) for information on the season of Easter.

Easter Sunday

The Scriptures for this day are the same for all three years. All suggestions are placed in Year A.

Second Sunday of Easter

Acts 4:32-35	To symbolize the sharing of possessions, place a variety of "possessions" on the table.
Psalm 133	A large circle or a wreath can symbolize the unity of this psalm.
1 John 1:1–2:2	Light is a theme for this reading. Consider a lamp that attaches to the head because this gives light on a path as you walk.
John 20:19-31 or Matthew 28:1-10	For these Scriptures you might use a cross with a large X across it, symbolizing resurrection and that Jesus' death was not final.

Third Sunday of Easter

Acts 3:12-19	Print out signs with the names of Abraham, Isaac, and Jacob on them. Place them on the draped table and then place a cross, symbolizing Jesus, over them.
Psalm 4	A large sign that says "Trust" would work well for this psalm.
1 John 3:1-7	This passage speaks of us as children of God. A picture of a child is appropriate here.
Luke 24:36b-48	Using a circle with a line through it and the word "Sin" in the center can symbolize that our sins are forgiven.

Fourth Sunday of Easter

Acts 4:5-12	Peter refers to Jesus as the stone that was rejected and became the cornerstone. Use a large square stone here. Or, if your emphasis is on the way the Holy Spirit worked through these men, then use a dove on the draped table. See page 37 for instructions on making a dove.
Psalm 23	This is such a familiar psalm. Of course a shepherd's crook is appropriate here.
1 John 3:16-24	To follow the theme of caring and loving others by our actions, use a heart and some symbol that represents one of your mission projects.
John 10:11-18	This passage can also be visualized with a shepherd's crook.

Fifth Sunday of Easter

Acts 8:26-40	This passage speaks of witnessing for Christ. Combine a symbol of some way that your church witnesses with the cross here.
Psalm 22:25-31	Use a globe and a cross to help the congregation visualize inclusiveness in this passage.
1 John 4:7-21	This speaks of love, and at the end adds that we must love our "brothers and sisters also." Using a heart is appropriate here. You might use the heart with a symbol of one of your church mission projects.
John 15:1-8	A cutting of a vine that branches out is appropriate here. Or you may use a potted vine that is branching.

Sixth Sunday of Easter

Acts 10:44-48	Use a dove and a bowl of water for this passage. See page 37 for instructions on making a dove.
Psalm 98	This psalm of praise has many visual images: God's hand, a lyre and trumpet, the sea, floods, and the hills. Any of these would be appropriate.
1 John 5:1-6	Combine a heart with a dove for this passage. See page 37 for instructions on making a dove.
John 15:9-17	The symbol of a heart can be used here. There is also reference to our bearing fruit, and so combine the heart with several missions that your church supports.

Seventh Sunday of Easter

Acts 1:15-17, 21-26	With a cross here, either use a dove or an image of flames representing the Holy Spirit. See page 37 for instructions on making a dove.
Psalm 1	The theme of this psalm is the two paths that we can choose to take. Therefore a picture of a split path may be used here. Or you can create a split path using the method suggested for the second Sunday of Advent for Year B.
1 John 5:9-13	A wreath of some sort and a cross can be used here. The wreath symbolizes eternity, and the cross Christ.
John 17:6-19	In this reading, Jesus asks that his followers be blessed as they carry out his mission. The cross and the world may be used in this context.

YEAR B

PENTECOST

See Year A (page 60) for information on the season of Pentecost. We use red on Pentecost Sunday and then change to green.

Day of Pentecost

Acts 2:1-21	This reading suggests two symbols to use here, the flame and a symbol of wind. You might hang a wind chime and place a small fan nearby so that it will chime quietly. Or a more modern image of wind would be the wind turbines. Also check with years A and C because the same Scripture is used there.
Psalm 104:24-34, 35b	This reading is the same as for Year A where we suggest using figures of people, animals, and such to surround the Bible and symbolize God as creator of ALL. Or you might simply use one flower or a picture of the face of a baby. Also check Year C because the same Scripture is used there.
Romans 8:22-27	Create a visual with the globe and a dove above it to symbolize the Holy Spirit's help throughout the world. See page 37 for instructions on making a dove.

John 15:26-27;
16:4b-15

Here again, the symbol of the dove may be used to represent the "Advocate" or the Holy Spirit. See page 37 for instructions on making a dove.

Trinity Sunday or First Sunday after Pentecost

The color for Trinity Sunday is white.

Isaiah 6:1-8

Using bright red tagboard, cut out the letters for the words "Here am I" and dramatically arrange them on a white drape. This represents Isaiah's call.

Psalm 29

A picture of a storm may be used for this reading.

Romans 8:12-17

A picture of children of different nationalities would be appropriate here, representing the unity statement that we are all children of God.

John 3:1-17

The familiar verse (John 3:16) is a part of this reading. This verse may be visualized with a globe or a map of the world and a large heart. However, if your emphasis for this reading is on our being renewed in the Spirit, you may use a baptismal bowl, which represents our new life in Christ.

YEAR B

ORDINARY TIME (AFTER PENTECOST)

See Year A (page 62) for information on Ordinary Time.

Second Sunday after Pentecost

1 Samuel 8:4-20 (11:14-15)	To represent Israel's request for a king, use a crown.
Psalm 138	This is a psalm of praise, but it also speaks of walking with God and God's love even in the midst of trouble. Use a thorny plant or a grouping of thorny vines with a cross placed over it.
2 Corinthians 4:13–5:1	This passage about not looking at what can be seen but the unseen may be symbolized with a mirror that has a large X across it and a heart beside it.

Mark 3:20-35

If the theme for today is on the first half of the reading, you may use a picture of a large house and cut the picture in two. Or you may involve teens and ask them to build two identical halves of a house out of Lego blocks. Lay the halves on their sides as if they have fallen because they were not whole.

The last verses speak of Jesus' statement about those around him as his brothers and sisters. If this theme is used, place a picture of people from many diverse ethnic groups on the table.

Third Sunday after Pentecost

1 Samuel 15:34–16:13

This Scripture tells of Samuel anointing David. A horn usually held oil for such an anointing, so this might be used. Or if you have services of anointing you might use whatever vessel you normally use for that oil. Placing some symbols of various ministries of your church might also be placed on the table, representing the calling that your laity has to teaching, worship leadership, mission, and such. If volunteers work in the kitchen or office or clean the facility, be sure to include symbols for those.

Psalm 20 or Psalm 92	For Psalm 20 a modern-day visual for a chariot might be a picture of an expensive car. Place the picture in a position that looks like it has fallen from a higher level, and then place a cross at the top. The beginning of Psalm 92 tells us to declare steadfast love in the morning and by night. Dual pictures of the same place both morning and night would be appropriate here. This psalm also speaks of bearing fruit in old age. The visual for the Mark reading below might be used here.
2 Corinthians 5:6-10 (11-13), 14-17	The last verse of this reading highlights the theme of change. This may be visualized with a rotting limb of a tree on the table and a small potted plant behind it as if it is growing from the composted tree branch. So that the pot does not show, you may cover it and part of the branch with pine straw or mulch.
Mark 4:26-34	Both parables in this reading deal with Jesus' message of witnessing or spreading the word as we spread seeds that grow. Arrange a number of seed packets. You might also add some "fruits" from those seeds, such as carrot seeds and a bunch of carrots.

Fourth Sunday after Pentecost

1 Samuel 17:(1a, 4-11, 19-23), 32-49	In David's example, we see a message of doing God's calling even if we seem unequipped. Use various items that represent mission work that your youth and children have done. Although David was probably a teenager when he was trusted with his father's sheep, children's ministries should be included in this representation.

Psalm 9:9-20	To represent this reading, use several play figures. Cover some with netting, but then pull the netting so that only a few are covered and secure the pulled netting to a cross.
2 Corinthians 6:1-13	To symbolize the obstacle or stumbling block that we should not place in another person's way, place a rock on the table and mark a large black X over it.
Mark 4:35-41	The storm being calmed in this reading can be depicted with two pictures, one of a storm at sea and one of a calm sea.

Fifth Sunday after Pentecost

2 Samuel 1:1, 17-27	This is a song of grief from David for Saul and Jonathan. A dark drape with large replicas of tears might be used here.
Psalm 130	Use the word "Redemption" in front of a picture of a glorious sunrise for this reading.
2 Corinthians 8:7-15	To portray the mission we're called to, use two images for this reading—one of what we have and one of people in need. The "what we have" image might be money, or it might be cans of food and clothing. The "people in need" image would be a picture of persons in need.
Mark 5:21-4	Use modern-day symbols of healing for this reading, such as medicine and bandages.

Sixth Sunday after Pentecost

2 Samuel 5:1-5, 9-10	This Scripture of David being made king can be shown with a royal colored drape (gold or purple) and a crown.
Psalm 48	Use the word "God" and a globe or map of the world here.
2 Corinthians 12:2-10	Use a large thorn, or a branch of thorns, and a cross to symbolize this reading where Paul says grace is sufficient in the midst of thorns.
Mark 6:1-13	Two pairs of sandals may be used for this reading. Place them as if they are walking their mission on a "road" made from a brown drape.

Seventh Sunday after Pentecost

2 Samuel 6:1-5, 12b-19	The joy of this occasion can be symbolized with bright streamers, tambourines (which were used then), and some sort of horn instrument.
Psalm 24	Build up a place in the center of the table and place a plaid drape over the entire table. Place a globe at the top. The plaid symbolizes all people woven together in unity, and the globe represents the earth.
Ephesians 1:3-14	Make a sign that says "Adopted" and place it across a picture of people from various diverse ethnic backgrounds.
Mark 6:14-29	Use a burlap drape (representing John the Baptist) for the table and very simply drape a black cloth across the burlap.

Eighth Sunday after Pentecost

2 Samuel 7:1-14a	A replica of a tent can be used here, symbolizing how God went with the Israelites as they moved from place to place.
Psalm 89:20-37	Prepare a "family tree" placing David's name at the bottom and Jesus' name on the top branch. You need not fill in the other names. The tree itself simply points to the lineage.
Ephesians 2:11-22	Here we might use a cornerstone, or simply a large word "One" over the cross.
Mark 6:30-34, 53-56	This reading speaks of Jesus as teacher. Placing teacher symbols around a cross may be a way to visualize this Scripture.

Ninth Sunday after Pentecost

2 Samuel 11:1-15	This reading tells of a big mistake that David made. Use a sign that says, "Mistake = Learning."
Psalm 14	Make a sign with some words of ungodliness (such as hate, murder, lying, and such) and place a large X over the whole sign.
Ephesians 3:14-21	Praying hands with the word "Faith" placed over them may be used here.
John 6:1-21	Use five small loaves of bread and two fish for this passage to represent the servanthood and caring of a small boy.

Tenth Sunday after Pentecost

2 Samuel 11:26–12:13a	For this, place one lone replica of a sheep on the table.
Psalm 51:1-12	See Ash Wednesday suggestions for this psalm.
Ephesians 4:1-16	Use a "gingerbread man" figure here and write "One" in large letters.
John 6:24-35	A large loaf of bread is appropriate here.

Eleventh Sunday after Pentecost

2 Samuel 18:5-9, 15, 31-33	David grieved not only for his son, but for what he had done. Display a picture of a man grieving.
Psalm 130	For redemption, use a crown of thorns and/or three large spikes.
Ephesians 4:25–5:2	Use the words "Kindness" and "Forgiving" here.
John 6:35, 41-51	A loaf of bread can be used here with a picture of Christ.

Twelfth Sunday after Pentecost

1 Kings 2:10-12; 3:3-14	To symbolize wisdom, use an open Bible with a pair of glasses on it.
Psalm 111	The word "awe" is often used for "fear" in this passage. Place this word on the table with a drape of gold.
Ephesians 5:15-20	A heart with a music note may be used here.
John 6:51-58	Use a loaf of bread and a chalice.

Thirteenth Sunday after Pentecost

1 Kings 8:(1, 6, 10-11), 22-30, 41-43	Use a picture of your church and place pictures of people from many diverse ethnic backgrounds around the church picture, representing verses 41-43.
Psalm 84	Use a picture of your church here, representing God's house.
Ephesians 6:10-20	A piece of armor for protection is appropriate here. You might use a bulletproof vest as a modern version of this, or a bright orange hunting vest.
John 6:56-69	Bread and chalice are appropriate here, too. Or you might use the words "Chosen by God" or "Called by God" in a banner or sign.

Fourteenth Sunday after Pentecost

Song of Solomon 2:8-13	To visualize this reading, use a display of flowers.
Psalm 45:1-2, 6-9	Use a stringed instrument on a gold drape.
James 1:17-27	Use symbols that represent mission work that your church participates in.
Mark 7:1-8, 14-15, 21-22	Use a heart, symbolizing that what is inside is important.

Fifteenth Sunday after Pentecost

Proverbs 22:1-2, 8-9, 22-23	Ahead of time, invite persons to bring something for your missions, food items for a food pantry, or such. As they come, ask them to place the food items on the draped table.

Psalm 124	To depict deliverance, use a large rope. Make it obvious that the ends of the rope are not tied.
James 2:1-10 (11-13) 14-17	To depict riches and poverty, use a gold drape and a burlap drape.
Mark 7:24-37	Use medical items here.

Sixteenth Sunday after Pentecost

Proverbs 1:20-33	A pair of glasses placed on the open Bible can symbolize wisdom.
Psalm 19	Use a gold drape and place an open Bible on it.
James 3:1-12	Use the bit for a horse or a ship replica here.
Mark 8:27-38	On a white drape, place a cross so that one arm of the cross is above and the other on the table, as if someone could step under the cross and lift it to the shoulder and follow Jesus' calling.

Seventeenth Sunday after Pentecost

Proverbs 31:10-31	A picture of a woman with her children is appropriate here. Using a picture with only the mother is inclusive of single mothers.
Psalm 1	Use a fresh branch from a tree—not wilted.
James 3:13–4:3, 7-8a	Use a dove or the peace sign here. See page 37 for instructions on making a dove.
Mark 9:30-37	Use pictures of children from your church to create a visual for verses 36 and 37.

Eighteenth Sunday after Pentecost

Esther 7:1-6, 9-10; 9:20-22	Display two pictures, one of sadness and one of joy.
Psalm 124	Sign: "Blessed be the name of the LORD."
James 5:13-20	Use a picture or figure of praying hands.
Mark 9:38-50	Use a block (stumbling block) or a millstone here.

Nineteenth Sunday after Pentecost

Job 1:1; 2:1-10	Make sign: "Upright Man."
Psalm 26 or Psalm 25	Use a picture of a straight path.
Hebrews 1:1-3; 2:5-12	To depict unity here, use a picture of people of all ages and place the words "Brothers and Sisters in Christ" across it.
Mark 10:2-16	Use pictures of children from diverse ethnic groups.

Twentieth Sunday after Pentecost

Job 23:1-9, 16-17	Use a picture of a brilliant sun, and place a black drape across the middle of it.
Psalm 22:1-15	Use a picture of a caring mother, cradling a child in her arms.
Hebrews 4:12-16	Place an open Bible here. If it is an adult gathering, you may want to use a "two-faced" sword, but do not use it if children are present.

Mark 10:17-31	Use the words "First" and "Last" and place arrows from one to the other, in both directions.

Twenty-first Sunday after Pentecost

Job 38:1-7 (34-41) Psalm 104:1-9, 24, 35c	For both of these readings, use a picture of the earth from space or a globe.
Hebrews 5:1-10	Use a picture of Jesus and a clergy stole (the Protestant equivalent of a priesthood symbol).
Mark 10:35-45	To depict how we must sometimes sacrifice to take the cup that Jesus takes, use a large chalice—or a more modern symbol would be a large coffee cup.

Twenty-second Sunday after Pentecost

Job 42:1-6, 10-17	Use the word "Blessings."
Psalm 34:1-8 (19-22)	A bowl of sugar or honey can symbolize verse 8.
Hebrews 7:23-28	Use an open Bible and a clergy stole (the Protestant equivalent of a priesthood symbol).
Mark 10:46-52	Place a coat casually on the draped table symbolizing in a modern way how we cast aside our coats in our haste to come to Christ. Or you might use a blindfold that is casually placed on the table.

Twenty-third Sunday after Pentecost

Ruth 1:1-18	Use an origami crane (known for its loyalty to its mate) for this reading. You can find instructions for making it at: http://www. origami-fun.com/origami-crane.html.
Psalm 146	Use a scale, representing justice.
Hebrews 9:11-14	To signify Christ's sacrifice, place a rugged cross on a pure white drape.
Mark 12:28-34	Use words: "Love God and neighbor."

Twenty-fourth Sunday after Pentecost

Ruth 3:1-5; 4:13-17	Use a Jesse tree or bare roots, symbolizing Jesse as the root of Jesus.
Psalm 42	Print "Hope" on a rock and place it on the table.
Hebrews 9:24-28	Place a cross on a bright yellow drape to represent Christ's sacrifice.
Mark 12:38-44	First use a piece of burlap covering for the table. Build up the center and place a white drape from top to bottom across the built-up center. Then place an empty offering plate in the center, tilted to show two shiny copper pennies in the plate, representing the sacrifice of the woman.

Twenty-fifth Sunday after Pentecost

1 Samuel 1:4-20	Use the picture of a baby with a wrapped gift beside it.
Psalm 16	Use a heart with "Rejoice" written on it.
Hebrews 10:11-14 (15-18) 19-25	Use a basin of water and towel.

Mark 13:1-8   Use stones that can be stacked, but scatter them across the table.

Thanksgiving Day

The suggested colors for this day are red and green. Check the other years for additional Thanksgiving ideas.

Joel 2:21-27   For both of these readings, place fruits
Psalm 126   of harvest on the table, full and spilling over.

1 Timothy 2:1-7   Use a Bible and a chain. Place them as if the Bible had been chained, but the chain is broken.

Matthew 6:25-33   Nestle a bird in a "nest" of brown drape.

Christ the King/Reign of Christ

White and gold are the colors for this special day.

2 Samuel 23:1-7   Place a wooden gavel on an open Bible, symbolizing how God can rule through those in charge.

Psalm 132:1-12   Use a lamp to symbolize the last verses of the
(13-18)   psalm.

Revelation 1:4b-8   Use the Greek letters Alpha and Omega.

John 18:33-37   Stain a white cloth with spots of red. Drape it over the table and then place a crown on it. This can remind us of the sacrifice Jesus made for what he believed.

Year C

ADVENT

See Year A (page 27) for information on Advent. We use purple or blue during this season.

First Sunday of Advent

Jeremiah 33:14-16	Use a branch of a tree for this reading, representing the prophecy of a righteous branch. The branch need not have leaves on it, in fact, the meaning will be clearer if there are no leaves.
Psalm 25:1-10	A picture or a model of a path would help the worshipers visualize this passage.
1 Thessalonians 3:9-13	This reading speaks of the love among the early Christians. A heart symbolizes that love.
Luke 21:25-36	You may use images of the sun, moon, and stars for this reading. Since this passage also includes the lesson of the fig tree, if you have access to fig leaves you may use these.

Second Sunday of Advent

Malachi 3:1-4	For this passage you may either follow the theme of the messenger or of the refiner. A messenger's cap may be used. If you use the theme of the refiner, find a rock that has mica in it. This gives the impression of a rock with silver or gold in it.
Luke 1:68-79	This prophecy of Zechariah speaks of John as the forerunner or messenger of Jesus. The messenger hat may be appropriate here too, but place it on a drape of burlap that would symbolize John the Baptist. To symbolize verses 78-79, use pictures of sunrise and darkness side by side.
Philippians 1:3-11	In this prayer Paul prays for the hearts of the Philippians to overflow with love. A large heart with "Love" will make a good visual.
Luke 3:1-6	Use the drape of burlap here, and for a modern-day image you might add a megaphone.

Third Sunday of Advent

All of the readings for this Sunday reflect joy, victory, and our response out of that joy. You may symbolize all of the Scriptures with the use of the word "Joy."

Zephaniah 3:14-20	Although this was written about Jerusalem, a modern-day picture of a major disaster (such as a tornado or earthquake) with the word "Victory" over it would help visualize this today.
Isaiah 12:2-6	Large letters spelling out the word "Joy" may be used to visualize this passage.
Philippians 4:4-7	Praying hands may be used here as a visual.

Luke 3:7-18	If you collect food for the hungry or items for some other mission during Advent, arrange some of it on the table. Invite those bringing contributions to place them on the table. During the Christmas season, too much emphasis is placed on receiving. Take this opportunity to stress giving.

Fourth Sunday of Advent

Micah 5:2-5a	This prophecy about Bethlehem may be portrayed with a picture of the city of Bethlehem. Or you may use a dove to symbolize the statement about peace at the end of the reading. See page 37 for instructions on making a dove.
Psalm 89:1-4, 19-26	Use a branch or a root here with a crown added, symbolizing that the ancestry of David's crown of power extended through the generations to Christ.
Hebrews 10:5-10	Although it seems inappropriate for the Advent season, the cross with a crown of thorns over it can be used here. This visual and this Scripture will help us connect the baby Jesus with the man Jesus and his sacrifice.
Luke 1:39-45 (46-55)	The meeting of Mary and Elizabeth and Mary's statement may be simply symbolized by placing a light blue drape over a darker blue or purple drape, Elizabeth being the darker (older) and Mary the lighter (younger).

Christmas Eve

The Scriptures for this day are the same for all three years. All suggestions are placed in Year A.

YEAR C

CHRISTMAS

See Year A (page 32) for information of the season of Christmas. We use white, yellow or gold.

Christmas Sunday/Christmas Day

The Scriptures for this day are the same for all three years. All suggestions are placed in Year A.

First Sunday after Christmas Day

1 Samuel 2:18-20, 26	This reading speaks of how Samuel helped in the temple. Place an acolyte robe on the table as a modern symbol of how children help lead us in worship.
Psalm 148	Use children's play figures here, including animals, trees, and people. You may also add a replica of the sun, moon, and stars. This Scripture is used in the first Sunday after Christmas in years A and B also. Check those suggestions.
Colossians 3:12-17	Verse 17 admonishes us to do everything in the name of Jesus. Place several everyday items on the table to indicate that we are called to follow Christ is all areas of our lives.

Luke 2:41-52   To symbolize the last verse of this passage, use a yardstick or a measuring device for children, some school books, and the Bible. By using today's images, we recognize that Jesus grew just as we grow today.

Second Sunday after Christmas Day

The Scriptures for this day are the same for all three years. All suggestions are placed in Year A.

Watch Night/New Year's Eve

The Scriptures for this day are the same for all three years. All suggestions are placed in Year A.

YEAR C

EPIPHANY

See Year A (page 36) for information on the season of Epiphany. We begin with white and change to green.

Epiphany Sunday

The Scriptures for this day are the same for all three years. All suggestions are placed in Year A.

Baptism of the Lord/First Sunday after the Epiphany

Isaiah 43:1-7	Use a globe or map of the world and the words "Called by Name."
Psalm 29	This Scripture speaks of the voice of God calling in the midst of a storm, bringing peace. Use a picture of a storm and the word "Peace."
Acts 8:14-17 Luke 3:15-17, 21-22	Use a dove as a symbol of the Holy Spirit for the reading from Acts and also the Gospel reading for this day. See page 37 for instructions on making a dove.

YEAR C

ORDINARY TIME (AFTER EPIPHANY)

See Year A (page 38) for information on Ordinary Time. Green is the color of this season.

Second Sunday after the Epiphany

Isaiah 62:1-5   Place a bridal veil across the green drape, showing God's delight in Israel.

Psalm 36:5-10   A picture of clouds may symbolize this reading. Or you might use any of the other images referenced here: mountains, oceans, river, or light.

1 Corinthians 12:1-11   Use various images to symbolize gifts that are used in the missions and ministries of your church. These may include a hammer, paintbrush, knitting needles, a piece of children's curriculum, a game you would play with youth, the Bible, food and medical items. These may all be placed on an infant's blanket that you use as a drape.

John 2:1-11   Large stone jars can be used for this passage. Or for a modern-day symbol, use a display of stemmed glasses.

Third Sunday after the Epiphany

Nehemiah 8:1-3, 5-6, 8-10 Psalm 19	Both Old Testament readings speak of the law of the Lord. For this theme, place a large Bible in a significant place on the table.
1 Corinthians 12:12-31a	From a large sheet of posterboard cut a "gingerbread man" type figure. On it place the names of various countries of today. Do not put the United States in a significant place. Be sure that you include the countries where your church supports missions. Also include countries that are in political unrest.
Luke 4:14-21	Use a long piece of paper and roll it at both ends to resemble a scroll. On the top of the scroll, where it can be seen, write "Isaiah."

Fourth Sunday after the Epiphany

Jeremiah 1:4-10	Place various symbols of ministry of your church and use the words "Called to Ministry."
Psalm 71:1-6	A large, unique rock can be used to symbolize God as our rock of refuge and hope.
1 Corinthians 13:1-13	The typical symbol for this passage is something to do with love, such as a heart. For something to stir thoughts about the contrasts, place a large gong or noise maker on one side of the table. Make a large X from posterboard, and paint it black. Place this on the gong or noise maker. Then on the other side of the table place a simple cross.
Luke 4:21-30	Use the scroll that you made for the Luke passage last week. Place a dove above it. See page 37 for instructions on making a dove.

Fifth Sunday after the Epiphany

Isaiah 6:1-13	Use a green drape as the background, and place a gold drape across it, draped from a higher point to the table. On the lower parts of the drape place the word "Holy" several times. Leave the higher part of the gold drape empty, signifying that we do not worship an image but the one true God.
Psalm 138	Use signs of different color and with different styles of writing with the word "Thanks."
1 Corinthians 15:1-11	The word "Grace" is appropriate for this reading. Use it as a visual in any way that you like.
Luke 5:1-11	Use a fishing net as a drape over a blue drape. Under the fishing net, place a globe, symbolizing our mission to spread the gospel to the world.

Sixth Sunday after the Epiphany

Jeremiah 17:5-10 Psalm 1	The visual image of trees planted by streams of water in both of these readings can be symbolized with a fresh limb of a tree, or smaller branches placed in a large glass vase so that the water is visible.
1 Corinthians 15:12-20	Use an empty tomb representation for this reading. You may plan ahead of time and ask an older elementary class to prepare one from clay, or ask the youth to build one out of Lego blocks.

Luke 6:17-26 — Jesus' message contrasts his followers with the prophets of their ancestors. By using the theme of following in the footsteps of the prophets, you can place a rough fabric drape and a pair of sandals on the table.

Seventh Sunday after the Epiphany

Genesis 45:3-11, 15 — Joseph chooses to make peace instead of taking revenge for the injustices the brothers laid on him. To visualize this, drape a fabric, striped with many colors, and place a dove of peace on it. Although some scholars of Genesis 37:3 translate Joseph's coat that he wore when his brothers put him in the pit and sold him as a "long robe with sleeves," the common memory of this story is a coat of many colors. See page 37 for instructions on making a dove.

Psalm 37:1-11, 39-40 — In Hebrew, the word for God, YHWH appears again in this psalm. The writer urges us to be patient and wait on the Lord (YHWH). A kitchen timer is often used to help children wait for an event. Place a large timer and a sign with YHWH on the table. Explain the translation of YHWH and the symbolism of the timer in the sermon or a printed medium.

1 Corinthians 15:35-38, 42-50 — To emphasize the contrast Paul gives in verse 42, place a variety of seed packets (the physical that is sown) on one side of the table and place a cross (the spiritual) on the other side.

Luke 6:27-38 — The theme of love and forgiveness climaxes in verses 37 and 38. To visualize the reading, place two identical clear containers on the table. Leave one empty and fill the other with some items so that it is full and spilling over. You might use grapes or some other fruit, blooms of flowers, pennies, or even assorted beads.

Eighth Sunday after the Epiphany

Isaiah 55:10-13 — Three possible images come to mind with this reading. You might emphasize the reference to bread as the word of God by using a loaf of bread. Or to crystallize verse 13, place a mass of thorny vines on the table and then place a live branch on top of it. An evergreen branch can symbolize God as ever life-giving. For another suggestion place a full plate of cookies on one side of the table and an identical plate empty on the other, reminding us that when someone gives us something (such as cookies) we return the plate with another gift (different cookies).

Psalm 92:1-4, 12-15 — Place an assortment of musical instruments on the table to illustrate verses 1-4. A palm branch and/or a large rock can illustrate verses 12-15 of this reading.

1 Corinthians 15:51-58 — In this reading, Paul speaks of how we will all be changed. Use a large replica of a butterfly for this, or a picture of a caterpillar and a butterfly. We have come to recognize the butterfly as a symbol of change.

Luke 6:39-49	If your theme emphasizes the first part of this reading, place a small log on the table. If you emphasize verses 46-49, place a stone on one side of the table and a pile of sand on the other.

Last Sunday after Epiphany/Transfiguration Sunday

The color for this Sunday is white.

Exodus 34:29-35	Light of some sort is appropriate for Transfiguration Sunday. The Exodus passage speaks of the light as the essence of the presence of God.
Psalm 99	This psalm speaks of the Lord as king over all the earth. Consider using a dazzling white drape with a gold drape coming from above and draping across the table with a globe set on the gold drape on the table.
2 Corinthians 3:12–4:2	Although light is evident in this Scripture, we might also represent it with a mirror and a veil draped over the mirror, as if moved aside.
Luke 9:28-36 (37-43)	Again, we find light as the major image in Luke's telling of the transfiguration. For a dramatic use of white, place white flowers in a white vase on a white drape.

Year C

LENT

See Year A (page 44) for information on the season of Lent. We use purple for this season.

Ash Wednesday

The Scriptures for this day are the same for all three years. All suggestions are placed in Year A.

First Sunday in Lent

Deuteronomy 26:1-11	A display of first fruits as gifts can include first fruits other than those from the earth. You might include a book, a miniature house, a pad and pencil, or anything else that can represent the vocations of those who are members of your congregation.
Psalm 91:1-2, 9-16	An angel may be used for this reading.
Romans 10:8b-13	Use the words, "Call on the name of the Lord."
Luke 4:1-13	A stone and a loaf of bread may suggest the first temptations of Christ. A royal crown might also be a part of this visual.

Second Sunday in Lent

Genesis 15:1-12, 17-18	Two images come to mind in this passage. You may use a shield, as God promised to be Abram's shield or protection. The other image is a picture of the canopy of the heavens with stars.
Psalm 27	This psalm often references strength. Body-building equipment may be used here. Or if you emphasize the protectiveness of God, make a small tent, as the psalmist refers to being sheltered by God's tent.
Philippians 3:17–4:1	Paul calls us to stand firm in the Lord, following the example of those before us. Use a fabric of woven colors, representing the spiritual ancestry of those who have woven the faith before us. Drape the fabric from a higher point to the table. Then place a cross on it, propped on the higher point.
Luke 13:31-35	Jesus used the illustration of a hen caring by protecting her brood. A picture of a hen, settled down, is appropriate here.

Third Sunday in Lent

Isaiah 55:1-9 Psalm 63:1-8	The Isaiah passage begins with the words, " . . . come to the waters." The passage from the Psalms also references the relief of water. A fountain would be a good choice for either, or if a fountain is not available, consider a picture of a waterfall. In the theme we find relief in God.
1 Corinthians 10:1-13	Paul references Christ as the rock in this reading. Use a rock and place a cross on the rock.

Luke 13:1-9 — Place a bowl of figs on the table to visualize the parable in this reading.

Fourth Sunday in Lent

Joshua 5:9-12 — Use unleavened bread and fruits to visualize this reading.

Psalm 32 — Use the words "Steadfast love" on a draped table.

2 Corinthians 5:16-21 — Here Paul speaks of change by being made new. Use two like objects (shoe, ball, towel, or such) one old and the other new. Place the old one on the table to one side. On the other side place the new object with a cross over it, symbolizing how Christ makes us a new person.

Luke 15:1-3,11b-32 — This parable is more about the father, or God's forgiveness, than the son. Rembrandt's famous painting *The Prodigal Son* might be used here. You can find the painting at http://www.rembrandtpainting.net/.

Fifth Sunday in Lent

Isaiah 43:16-21 — To emphasize the change to a better way that God plans, make two paths in a bed of sand. On one place stones and thorns. Make the other clear, as if it were just created.

Psalm 126 — To represent the joy suggested here, use a sheaf of wheat. If that's not available, consider a display of vegetables and grain.

Philippians 3:4b-14	Place a sign above the table that reads "Goal" and on the table place the cross to symbolize Christ as our goal.
John 12:1-8	Place a large bottle that might hold perfume or an expensive oil on the table. Beside it place a pile of money.

Sixth Sunday in Lent (Passion/Palm Sunday)

Liturgy of the Palms

Luke 19:28-40	Use palm branches throughout the church, on the floor in the hallway and leading to the front of the sanctuary.
Psalm 118:1-2, 19-29	Add a large stone to palm branches on the table, symbolizing the cornerstone.

Liturgy of the Passion

Isaiah 50:4-9a Psalm 31:9-16 Philippians 2:5-11	These Scriptures are the same for all three years. All suggestions are placed in Year A.
Luke 22:14–23:56 (or Luke 23:1-49)	These Scriptures give the whole Passion. You may use several symbols, including: bread and cup (Last Supper); money bag and coins (Judas's betrayal); rooster (Peter's denial); crown of thorns (before Pilate); whip (flogging); three large nails and hammer (crucifixion).

Monday through Saturday of Holy Week

The Scriptures for these days are the same for all three years. All suggestions are placed in Year A.

Year C

EASTER

See Year A (page 54) for information on the season of Easter. The color for this season is white.

Easter Sunday

Many of these passages are the same for all years. See other years for suggestions.

Acts 10:34-43 or Jeremiah 31:1-6
Psalm 118:1-2, 14-24
1 Corinthians 15:19-26 or Acts 10:34-43

From Insect Lore (www.livebug.com) order a butterfly garden in time for the butterflies to hatch on Easter morning. Hang the garden. Add flowering branches.

John 20:1-18

Construct a tomb with rocks or blocks and have the entrance open wide. In the opening, place a white cloth draped on down to the floor. You may choose to have a children's or youth class make the tomb.

Luke 24:1-12	Many symbols are used for the resurrection of Jesus, particularly symbols that show new life from something that appears dead or without life, such as eggs, butterflies, and lilies. For something different, use a drab background drape and take several pieces of white sheeting. Some may be folded neatly and some may be cast aside as if someone pushed them aside.

Second Sunday of Easter

Acts 5:27-32	On the display, prop open a large Bible and have a title sign next to it that reads, "We are witnesses to these things."
Psalm 118:14-29	Use a gate opened wide. Decorate the area around the gate with blooming flowers and plants.
Revelation 1:4-8	Use the symbols for Alpha and Omega. Make them out of dazzling foils or lights. Place them against a dark backdrop.
John 20:19-31	Display a door. If possible, use a door that is still on its frame and hinged. Prop the door open and place a sign on the door that says, "I am still with you."

Third Sunday of Easter

Acts 9:1-6, 7-20	There are many posters and illustrations that can be found in curriculum pieces of the conversion of Paul. Use one of these on an easel.

Psalm 30	To illustrate the beautiful phrase, "You have turned my mourning into dancing" drape the table with a black cloth. Then sprinkle with silver streamers and glitter. As the focal point place a pair of white ballet slippers or toe shoes in the middle.
Revelation 5:11-14	In one of many possible ways, use your display area to show as many angels as possible. You might consider scattering small photographs of members of your church among the angels as well.
John 21:1-19	Make a display of fishing props. Use a fishing net draped on the table then add a fishing rod, basket and fish. Also add a large loaf of bread.

Fourth Sunday of Easter

Acts 9:36-43	Place a mirror on display with the words "We shall be like Christ" written on it.
Psalm 23 Revelation 7:9-17	"The LORD is my shepherd" from Psalm 23 and the reference of Christ the shepherd in Revelation can both be illustrated with an image, a painting, or a sculpture of a shepherd and flock of sheep.
John 10:22-30	Although this Scripture speaks of Jesus and God as one, it does begin to move toward the concept of the Trinity. Meditation of the oneness of God and Christ and even the Spirit can be represented with one of the many symbols of the Trinity.

Fifth Sunday of Easter

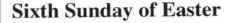

Acts 11:1-18 — There is a phrase that speaks of unity, "All Means All." Those three words written and displayed will cause many to contemplate.

Psalm 148 — Not just the heavens, but all of creation is praised in the song. To symbolize all of God's universe, use a poster of a nebula or a galaxy full of glory for the display. This Scripture is also used in the first Sunday after Christmas for all three years. Check those suggestions.

Revelation 21:1-6 — If there is electricity available, use a tabletop fountain to symbolize the spring of the water of life.

John 13:31-35 — Such a beautiful message of love can be well represented with an abundance of hearts, valentines, and "kisses" candies. Don't forget to hand out the candies after the service.

Sixth Sunday of Easter

Acts 16:9-15 — Use a basket full of purple clothes, representing Lydia who became a believer in this text. Use many different hues, textures, and designs but all shades of purple.

Psalm 67 — A globe may be used to indicate all nations singing for joy before the Lord in this reading.

Revelation 21:10, 22–22:5 — Place a tree in the middle of the display. A small ficus tree works well. At the base of the tree spread several of twelve different kinds of fruit, indicating the healing of the nations.

John 14:23-29   Jesus' gift to his disciples just prior to his death was a word of prophecy, hope, and peace. To symbolize the strong message of peace, display one of the many peace signs recognizable today.

Ascension Sunday

Acts 1:1-11   Encourage people to ponder the time of the Lord by placing a large clock on display.

Psalm 47   Use many symbols and items of music for the display. Sheet music and a shiny trumpet can be the props. Adorn with streamers and confetti.

Ephesians 1:15-23   The first chapter of Ephesians, including the verses of this reading, makes reference to the many gifts we have in Christ. Place a grouping of beautifully wrapped gifts as the display to represent wisdom, revelation, enlightenment, hope, riches, greatness, and the church.

Luke 24:44-53   Make a copy from a Bible map and place Jerusalem in the middle, enlarge and copy it on light brown or beige paper, as if it is old paper. Stick a large thumbtack at the Jerusalem location to mark its importance and the beginning point of witnessing to the world.

Seventh Sunday of Easter

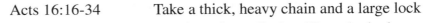

Acts 16:16-34	Take a thick, heavy chain and a large lock and drape it on display. Have the lock open. Perhaps display a key next to the lock. You might also have the chain broken. This represents freedom.
Psalm 97	This psalm is full of imagery from the natural world. Take a large poster or print of nature and display it on an easel.
Revelation 22:12-14, 16-17, 20-21	Make a large card and print "You are invited" on top and then the word "Come" below. All are invited to come.
John 17:20-26	Christ in us and God in Christ is a phrase of completeness and oneness. The symbol of the circle represents the same sort of unity. Make a large circle with lighted tea candles.

YEAR C

PENTECOST

See Year A (page 60) for information on Pentecost. The color for Pentecost is red.

Acts 2:1-21 or
Genesis 11:1-9

Make a collage, or place words in many different languages on a display board. The collage can be of diverse peoples. Or the words can all be the same word written in a variety of ways. Also check with years A and B because the same Scripture is used there.

Psalm 104:24-34, 35b

Take a red velvet cloth and drape it on the display. Place one of the many famous prints of the Day of Pentecost on a stand. Also check years A and B because the same Scripture is used there.

Romans 8:14-17
John 14:8-17 (25-27)

Label a pitcher with the words "Holy Spirit," and place it next to a simple figure of a human being. If you can adjust the pieces, have the pouring spout of the pitcher toward the figure. Use gold, silver, and white tinsel and glitter to connect the pitcher to the person.

Trinity Sunday or First Sunday after Pentecost

Proverbs 8:1-4, 22-31 Psalm 8	Displays of creation and the glory of the universe are perfect. Photos of space, nature scenes, and new birth of plants and animals all can be used.
Romans 5:1-5 John 16:12-15	Doves are wonderful symbols for the Holy Spirit. Ask a children's class to make doves and hang them. See page 37 for instructions to make doves.

YEAR C

ORDINARY TIME (AFTER PENTECOST)

See Year A (page 62) for information on Ordinary Time. Green is the color of this season.

Second Sunday after Pentecost

1 Kings 17:8-24	Enlarge a picture of Elijah from old curriculum materials or illustrated Bible stories. Title it with the words "God's special person. Do good things for God."
Psalm 146	Use music symbols or a piece of sheet music to share in the song of praise.
Galatians 1:11-24	God's revelation comes in many, many ways. For Paul, it was dramatic. For others, it comes quietly and slowly. Either way, a good symbol is light. Use a candle or lantern as the focus.
Luke 7:11-17	"Arise!" Write this word on helium balloons and display them.

Third Sunday after Pentecost

1 Kings 21:1-21a	Write the words "Lies" and "Cheat" on pieces of paper. Then, in red, mark through them with a big circle and slash symbolizing NO.
Psalm 5:1-8	"SOS" written out on a sign, a white flag, and a distress signal flag (orange with a black circle and square on it) all represent our cry for help.
Galatians 2:15-21	Write the word "Faith" in calligraphy and display it.
Luke 7:36–8:3	There is a print of Jesus and the biblical women in his life. If you can obtain it, use it for this reading. If not, a simple alabaster jar on display represents the importance of women in Jesus' life.

Fourth Sunday after Pentecost

1 Kings 19:1-15a	Take a very small tree or tree-shaped plant and display it with a small loaf of bread and a jar of water.
Psalm 42	Make a stack of smooth rocks, piled one on top of the other to symbolize the things we ponder in meditation.
Galatians 3:23-29	Make a large collage of diverse people . . . people of all shapes, colors, sizes, ages, gender, and ethnic origins. To emphasize unity, title the collage "One in Christ Jesus."
Luke 8:26-39	This Scripture is another story of healing. "Tormented and Now Healed" can be spelled out on a message board similar to what we see in front of stores.

Fifth Sunday after Pentecost

2 Kings 2:1-2, 6-14 — Tear an old, discarded coat in two pieces. Drape it on display so that it is still obviously a coat. Add to it a new mantle or cloak. If possible, hang it above the old as if it were descending.

Psalm 77:1-2, 11-20 — Display a large scrapbook. Add a title to the scrapbook that says "Scrapbook of Memories."

Galatians 5:1, 13-25 — Use old law books or make mock books by marking "Law" on them. Scatter the books about in a disruptive way. Have one book opened to a page of blank white paper with the only words written on it, "You shall love your neighbor as yourself."

Luke 9:51-62 — The focus is Jesus himself and our decision to follow him. Display a painting of Jesus with the words "Follow Me" draped on the painting. You can also use an illustration of footprints.

Sixth Sunday after Pentecost

2 Kings 5:1-14	Make gauze bandages look dirty, worn, and bloodied. Create a pile with these bandages. Add a small scroll next to them with the words "No longer a leper" written on it.
Psalm 30	Display a large, glorious painting or photograph of a sunrise. Title the display with verse 5b: " . . . but rejoicing comes in the morning."
Galatians 6:1-6 (7-16)	Spread good soil out over the display area. Make small crop markers and post them in the soil. Write on the markers words such as, "gentleness," "spirit," "goodness," "peace," and "new creation."
Luke 10:1-11, 16-20	Borrow one of your pastor's stoles and drape it with a Bible and anointing oil in a small jar to symbolize the ministry we do in the name of Christ. Jesus sent out the seventy messengers. We are still being called forth.

Seventh Sunday after Pentecost

Amos 7:7-17	Use not only a plumb line, but a couple other builder's tools as well. Add a yardstick, level, and carpenter's pencil, with the plumb line hanging as if in use.
Psalm 82	For this week and the next few weeks, the Psalter focuses on judgment as one of the characters of God. Use a scale of justice for the prop.

Colossians 1:1-14	A Christian life bears witness in the fruit it produces. This Scripture emphasizes the good works we do. Living the Christian life is something seen. Use a mirror as a meditative prop for this introspection.
Luke 10:25-37	The symbol for the American Red Cross is recognized universally for the help this organization gives to anyone in need. Use the symbol of the American Red Cross as a modern-day way of saying we care and are here to help.

Eighth Sunday after Pentecost

Amos 8:1-12	Fill a basket with fresh fruit. Then place some rotten and half eaten fruit outside the basket. And, finally, place an old core of an apple or pear away from the rest.
Psalm 52 or Psalm 82	Use the scale of justice to symbolize God's judgment.
Colossians 1:15-28	The symbols of the Alpha and Omega can be made out of foil and pinned on a dark backdrop.

Verses 26 and 27 speak of the mystery that is revealed. As a visual for these verses, consider using a puzzle map of the world with enough of the puzzle pieces in place to show that it is the world, but some pieces placed beside the map.

Luke 10:38-42	The use of old curriculum illustrations or a print of Mary and Martha with Jesus would be simple and to the point of this well-known story. Or you may illustrate the choices these women made by placing a cook pot and a Bible side by side on the draped table. In this story Jesus gave these women opportunities that were usually only open to men.

Ninth Sunday after Pentecost

Hosea 1:2-10	Create a small seascape with sand to represent the children of God. Make a sun umbrella from cardboard and fasten it to a small garden stake. On the umbrella write "Children of the living God."
Psalm 85	Use a set of children's building blocks that have letters on them to create a tower spelling out R-E-S-T-O-R-A-T-I-O-N. Or you may create larger blocks from cardboard with the letters.
Colossians 2:6-19	On a large, wooden cross nail a piece of paper with "Old Self" written on it.
Luke 11:1-13	Praying hands, a beautifully illustrated poster of the Lord's Prayer, or a child's craft project of hands folded in prayer would all make great displays of this lesson. (See Year A, Ash Wednesday.)

Tenth Sunday after Pentecost

Hosea 11:1-11 Psalm 107:1-9, 43	Use a weathervane to symbol the gathering of diverse people from all directions and places.
Colossians 3:1-11	"Christ is all and in all." Use this verse on unity as a title to a display representing a variety of peoples. It can be done as a collage.
Luke 12:13-21	Display a treasure chest overflowing with silver, gold, and jewels.

Eleventh Sunday after Pentecost

Isaiah 1:1, 10-20	Print out a checklist on a large piece of paper that lists the following: repent, cease doing evil, learn to do good, seek justice, rescue the oppressed, defend the orphan, and plead the case of the widow.
Psalm 50:1-8, 22-23	Depict a simple symbol of the judgment of God with a scale of justice.
Hebrews 11:1-3, 8-16	Post a picture of Abraham and Sarah on an easel. You might also make a caption that reads, "Faith of Our Ancestors."
Luke 12:32-40	Use a lit lamp as the focal point of your display to symbolize readiness and waiting.

Twelfth Sunday after Pentecost

Isaiah 5:1-7	Make a display using grape vines. Place them all over the display table or against a small section of fencing.
Psalm 80:1-2, 8-19	Use a large dead-looking branch that has one single green shoot on it and display. You can make one by taking any healthy branch and stripping it of all but one stem.
Hebrews 11:29–12:2	Use old curriculum pieces or copy pictures from a Bible storybook. Tear around dozens of faith leaders' pictures and make a big, busy collage that represents our faith ancestors. Or you may use a plaid cloth and reference each color as one of the ancestral witnesses mentioned in the text. If you use the plaid cloth, give each worshiper a small square of plaid fabric as a reminder of the faith heroes of their past and their obligation to become a witness of faith to new generations.
Luke 12:49-56	Take a large warning street sign and post it. You might also use a flashing yellow light if you have electricity at your display site.

Thirteenth Sunday after Pentecost

Jeremiah 1:4-10	Use a statue of a young boy to represent the story of young Jeremiah being called by God. This can be a modern-day boy.
Psalm 71:1-6	Construct a model fortress, or post a print of an ancient fort. A youth class might enjoy doing the construction project.

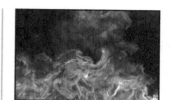

Hebrews 12:18-29 — A blazing fire would make a great symbol for this Scripture, but would no doubt be dangerous. However, there are nice artificial fire displays. One can also be made with a small fan aimed upward and hidden with logs. To the wire fan cover, tie short lengths of red, orange, and yellow streamers. The fan will blow them to look like flames.

Luke 13:10-17 — Place an empty wheelchair on display. In the seat you can place a big red heart. Another idea would be to place a sign in the seat that reads, "Healed on the Sabbath."

Fourteenth Sunday after Pentecost

Jeremiah 2:4-13
Psalm 81:1, 10-16 — A print of curriculum or church storybook of the Exodus would go nicely with these Scriptures. Or you may use a Bible open to Exodus. Place a jar of honey beside it.

Hebrews 13:1-8, 15-16 — Use a basin, pitcher, and towel as perfect symbols of hospitality and service.

Luke 14:1, 7-14 — Make paper dolls and stand them up by using a small ball of clay at the base of each one. Arrange them in a casual line moving from front to back. Place one more, a bit larger as the focal point, at the end of the line.

Fifteenth Sunday after Pentecost

Jeremiah 18:1-11	Borrow and set up a potter's wheel at your display area. You might also put an unfinished piece or a lump of clay on it. If you are unable to find a potter's wheel, use a large lump of clay and place a finished piece of pottery beside it.
Psalm 139:1-6, 13-18	Use a statue of a pregnant woman.
Philemon 1-21	Two important words: "Rejoice" and "Proclaim." Write them out and display them with a scattering of sheet music.
Luke 14:25-33	Make a display of blueprints, a legal pad, and a pencil. Write boldly across the pad "Plan."

Sixteenth Sunday after Pentecost

Jeremiah 4:11-12, 22-28	Make a display of a desert landscape. Pour sand as the foundation and add a piece of driftwood, lonely and bare.
Psalm 14	There is a New Testament verse, Mark 9:24, that ends with the phrase, "I do believe; help me overcome my unbelief!" This verse is a beautiful pairing to Psalm 14. Take that phrase, write it in calligraphy, and post.
1 Timothy 1:12-17	Take a photograph of your church, enlarge it, and display it on an easel. Title it, "This church welcomes sinners."

Luke 15:1-10 — Out of responsibility, diligence, and love, both the shepherd and the woman looked for the lost because even the least is of value. The focal point of the display can be a telescope or a large magnifying glass.

Seventeenth Sunday after Pentecost

Jeremiah 8:18–9:1
Psalm 79:1-9 or
Psalm 4
1 Timothy 2:1-7 — All three of these Scriptures speak to our reaction to times of trial as times we call out to God. We do this in prayer. Use praying hands as the focal point to the display.

Luke 16:1-13 — Make a big pile of paper currency and coins. Make three signs representing choices, "Save," "Live," and "Give."

Eighteenth Sunday after Pentecost

Jeremiah 32:1-3a, 6-15 — Make a vignette with a "sold" house sign, a deed and a judge's gavel.

Psalm 91:1-6, 14-16 — An armor shield is a powerful symbol of protection. Use a shield for the display.

1 Timothy 6:6-19
Luke 16:19-31 — God speaks to us through the stories of the Bible. The words are in black and white. Today there are still signs that we need to see. Consider using a collection of road signs for display.

Nineteenth Sunday after Pentecost

Lamentations 1:1-6 Psalm 137	These readings are songs of lamentation. To represent the sadness and the tears, drape the display area with a black cloth and set up a white actor's sad-faced mask.
2 Timothy 1:1-14	Paul speaks of faith in God as the most valuable treasure in life. Use a treasure chest as the focal point in the display.
Luke 17:5-10	If the theme is on the mustard seed, make a chart of different-sized seeds from the small mustard seed to a large tree seed. Emphasize the difference in sizes. You might give each person a seed as they enter the meeting place.

Twentieth Sunday after Pentecost

Jeremiah 29:1, 4-7	To symbolize the exile, the distant lands, the new homeland and sense of place, use a large map, a compass, and a small altar of stones stacked one on top of another to symbolize the people who moved to new lands and homes.
Psalm 66:1-12	This song is in praise for God's guidance in times of wandering and journey to the Promised Land. The display suggested above works here as well for this passage.

2 Timothy 2:8-15	Stay close to Christ Jesus is the message of this passage. If we draw close to Jesus in the hearing of his stories, then we can represent this in a display of the parables. Instead of the Bible, the focal point could be a book of parables or a book titled, "The New Testament" or "The Good Gospel."

Luke 17:11-19	Make two paper dolls, cut in such a way that a piece of paper in the shape of a square or rectangle is between the two dolls in their hands. Make them large enough so that they can easily be seen. On the square, or rectangle, write the words "Thank You."

Twenty-first Sunday after Pentecost

Jeremiah 31:27-34	Use a large piece of red paper to make a giant heart-shaped valentine. Write on it, "I will write it on their hearts." Add additional hearts or sprinkle heart candies around.
Psalm 119:97-104 or Psalm 19	Make a scroll of paper or construct model tablets. Then write on it, "The law of the Lord is perfect, trustworthy, right, radiant, pure, and sure."
2 Timothy 3:14–4:5	The importance of Scripture can be displayed in many ways. You might use a display of blocks with the name of a Bible book written on each block.

Luke 18:1-8	Take a door and prop it up in your display area. Attach a door knocker and a door handle if the door does not have them. Hang a sign on the door handle that says, "Keep knocking."

Twenty-second Sunday after Pentecost

Joel 2:23-32
Psalm 65

God provides in all circumstances, and this message is strongly conveyed in Joel's prophecy and the reading from the Psalter. A display of faith and perseverance can be accomplished with seeds, a watering can, soil, and an empty basket signifying the expected harvest.

2 Timothy 4:6-8, 16-18

Working hard, holding firm, and finishing the race stand out in this message. Use a pair of running shoes to symbolize the race, the perseverance, and the effort spoken in this message.

Luke 18:9-14

Enlarge a photo of your church and set it on an easel. Above the photo label the photo, "Sinners welcome here."

Twenty-third Sunday after Pentecost

Habakkuk 1:1-4; 2:1-4

Standing at watch, keeping an open eye, and sending messages can be represented with comfort in the symbol of the lighthouse.

Psalm 119:137-44

Dependence on the law and advice from God can be symbolized with a scroll or tablets. For a modern spin, arrange a stack of law books of today.

2 Thessalonians 1:1-4, 11-12

Take three body building pieces such as a dumbbell, a free weight, and a weighted ball to arrange as a symbol of staying strong in the faith.

Luke 19:1-10

You can depict this well-known story with an illustration of Zacchaeus in the tree. Look in curriculum pieces to find a poster of the story. If you cannot find an illustration, a tree branch will work as a symbol.

All Saints Day

White is used for All Saints Day.

Daniel 7:1-3, 15-18	For an abstract reference to dreams, consider using a photograph of clouds in the sky to represent the strange designs of our dreams.
Psalm 149 or Psalm 150	Both of these psalms begin with the exclamation, "Praise the LORD." That phrase boldly and beautifully written in a festive cursive declares the praise.
Ephesians 1:11-23	Paul earnestly prayed for the church. His prayers for the people were heartfelt. Use praying hands as the focus of this Scripture.
Luke 6:20-31	The Beatitudes and the Great Commandment are the message of this passage. Words such as "Blessed be" and "Do to others as you would have them do to you" written on a scroll of paper is a simple way to share the message.

Twenty-fourth Sunday after Pentecost

Haggai 1:15b–2:9	Use a good print of the Temple or build a model of the Temple for display. If building a model, a children's Sunday school class could do this project. A youth class might like to build the Temple with Lego blocks, or a simple way to do this is to use children's building blocks.
Psalm 145:1-5, 17-21	One important message in this reading is the call for one generation to witness or tell of God to the next generation. The importance of rejoicing and telling the stories is symbolized by the use of a totem pole or storytelling doll.
2 Thessalonians 2:1-5, 13-17	Any symbol of strength, such as armor, represents the message of standing firm and holding fast.
Luke 20:27-38	The hymn titled "And Are We Yet Alive" by Charles Wesley asks the same question as this Scripture verse. Use these words from the hymn title to display this question. This gives us thought of resurrection in our life today as well as the future.

Twenty-fifth Sunday after Pentecost

Isaiah 65:17-25	Consider taking the word "New" and create a display of hope for the future. Simply use the words "New heavens and new earth" or work with symbols of the new growth of seeds, stuffed-toy baby animals peacefully nestled together, or a print of a super nova exploding into creation.

Isaiah 12 or Psalm 118	Symbols of music represent the song in Isaiah. For the psalm, the words, "His steadfast love endures forever" written repeatedly with hearts as decorations make a nice display.
2 Thessalonians 3:6-13	This reading brings us the message that we should being doing the work of Christ. To symbolize the servant ministry of good works, use the basin and towel. Or you may display symbols from some of your church's mission projects.
Luke 21:5-19	Symbols for martyrdom may vary and may be difficult. But the bottom line can be represented with the crosses we all bear in the name of Christ. Use many, many crosses for a very impressive display.

Christ the King/Reign of Christ

Use the colors white or gold.

Jeremiah 23:1-6	Sheep and shepherds are mentioned throughout this Scripture. Images of a shepherd and sheep, a shepherd's crook, or a framed art piece of a flock works well here.
Luke 1:68-79	Symbols of salvation and rescue are appropriate. As in the Jeremiah reading, the traditional symbol of a shepherd works. A more modern symbol could be a life preserver or life ring.
Colossians 1:11-20	Christ is the beginning, the head, the first, and above all things. Make a big blue first place ribbon to display.
Luke 23:33-43	Recognition of Christ on the cross with two criminals being executed with him can be represented with a display of three crosses.

Thanksgiving Day

The colors green, white, or red are sometimes used here. Check the other years for additional Thanksgiving ideas.

Deuteronomy 26:1-11	Place an overflowing basket of fruits and vegetables on the display. Print on a wide ribbon, "a land flowing with milk and honey" and place it around the fruit.
Psalm 100	Make a display of musical symbols with sheet music, horns, bells, and the like to represent the concept of "coming before the Lord with joyful songs."
Philippians 4:4-9	Take a sheet of paper and title it, "Think About These Things." Then list the words true, honorable, just, pure, pleasing, commendable, excellence, and worthy of my praise in a column.
John 6:25-35	To represent the true bread of life that the Father gives, display a huge basket of breads. You could also include the words "Bread of Life" in the basket. Using various ethnic breads represents the "Bread of Life" being for ALL people.

WORKING NOTE CARDS

My notes:

A-ha ideas:

Supplies to collect:

Date used:

APPENDIX 2
RECORD KEEPING FORM

Item	Location	Person	Contact #	Date Used

Appendix 3
SYMBOLS

Seasonal Symbols

Season	Symbol	Meaning
Advent	Angels	Told of Christ's birth
Advent	Bells	Toll the news
Advent	Candles/light	Christ, the light of the world
Advent	evergreens and wreath	Eternal life
Advent	Manger/Nativity	Christ's birth
Advent	Star	Shone over stable
Advent	Trumpets	Announce birth
Epiphany	Crowns	Magi who came
Epiphany	Star	Led the magi
Lent	Ashes	Penitence
Lent	Bread and Chalice	Lord's Supper
Lent	Coins	Betrayal
Lent	Crown of thorns	Christ's torture
Lent	Palm	Life and victory
Lent	Whip	Christ's suffering
Easter	Butterfly	Death and resurrection
Easter	Lily	What appears dead has life
Easter	Egg	Life comes forth
Pentecost	Flame, wind, and dove	Holy Spirit

Sacramental Symbols	
Baptism	shell, water, dove
Communion	chalice, bread, wheat, grapes
Traditional Symbols	
Alpha and Omega	beginning and end
Basin and towel	service
Bible, scrolls	the Word of God
Candle/lamp	Christ, the light of the world
Circle	eternity, no beginning and no end
Cross	Christ's death for us
Fish	the Christian faith (as used by early Christians)
Lamb	Christ's sacrifice for sins
Rainbow	God's faithfulness
Rose, red	blood of Christ and martyrs
Rose, white	purity
Seeds	new life, resurrection and hope
Shepherd's crook	Christ as Good Shepherd
Ship	church, place of refuge
Sword	the struggle against evil
Triangle	the Trinity
Modern Symbols	
Angels	heavenly presence, prophecy, announcement
Aquarium or fish bowl	calm, the sea, community
Basin and pitcher	servant ministry, Jesus' act
Basket with food	abundance, provision,
Blueprints	plan, direction
Boots and shoes	journey, work, travel
Butterfly pavilion/live butterflies	new birth, Easter, resurrection
Camera with large lens	focus
Camping tent	wandering, journey
Candles	light, meditation, Christ

Modern Symbols	
Chrismons	Advent, Christmas, symbols of Christ
Clocks	time, preparedness
Coins	payment, value, cost
Compass	direction, journey
Crook and cane	shepherd, leader
Crown	Old Testament royalty
Cup and plate with bread	Eucharist/Communion
Doves	baptism, spirit
Eggs	new birth, Easter, resurrection
Eternity lamp	remembrance, cloud of witnesses
Fabric	(woven plaid or multicolors) diversity, heritage
Fish nets, oars	disciples
Fishing supplies, nets, oars	biblical stories, evangelism
Fruits and vegetables	abundance, provision when not using fresh produce
Gardening supplies, tools, soil, watering can, seed packets	growth, nurture
Gate section	path, journey, safekeeping, protection
Gifts beautifully wrapped	presents, abundance, gifts, talents
Glass pitcher and cup with water	water, drink, compassion, caring
Globe	concerns for the world, unity
Hearts	love, compassion
Icons (modern art)	meditation, story, people
Instruments	music, praise
Labyrinth (lap and stylus types)	journey, meditation
Lights and lamps	guidance, discipleship, Christ
Loom	diversity, heritage

Modern Symbols	
Menorahs	Jewish heritage
Mirror	sight, image
Mobiles of stars and planets	creation, God's universe
Nativity sets, crèches	Christmas, Jesus' birth narratives
Peace signs	peace
Pitcher	life-giving water, baptism
Plants, vines, tree stumps, roots	life, heritage
Pottery, potter's wheel, clay	creating, maturing, molding, parenting
Prints of religious art work/easel	meditation, story focus
Pump	water, provision
Quilts and fabrics	color and texture representing different ideas, ethnicity
Road signs, street signs	direction, message, attention
Rocks, stones, sand	altars, wilderness, foundation
Scrolls of paper	laws, lessons
Sheet music, instruments	music, song, joy, worship
Skeleton	bones, life and death
Stained glass window (small) on easel	meditation, story
Statues	designating specific people
Stones	altars, worship, dependable, strength
Street signs	direction, choice, journey
Stuffed animals	creation, Noah
Telescope, binoculars, magnifying glass	vision, search, sight
Totem pole	storytelling

Modern Symbols	
Treasure chest	gift, treasure
Vessels, earthen	broken and whole
Umbrella	protection
Wagon wheel	unity, connection, circle of life
Weather vanes	direction of the Spirit, direction
Weights of measure	justice, law
Well pump (old style)	water, provision
Works of art set on an easel	stories, people, imagery

TOPICAL INDEX

Topic	Year	Sunday/Season
Abundance	A	4th Easter; Thanksgiving Day
	C	5th Easter
Ancestry	B	4th Advent; 8th and 24th Pentecost
	C	4th Advent; 2nd Lent; 11th and 12th Pentecost
Baptism	A	1st Epiphany; 3rd Easter
	B	1st Epiphany; 1st Lent; 1st Pentecost
	C	1st Epiphany
Betrayal	A	Holy Week Friday
Calling	B	2nd and 3rd Epiphany; 1st, 3rd, 4th, 13th, and 16th Pentecost
	C	1st Christmas; 1st Epiphany; 6th and 13th Pentecost
Care	A	3rd Lent
	B	4th Easter; 19th & 20th Pentecost
	C	2nd Lent; 7th Pentecost
Change	B	3rd Pentecost
	C	8th Epiphany; 4th and 5th Lent
Choice/Decision	A	6th Epiphany; 3rd Pentecost
	B	7th Easter
	C	5th, 8th, and 17th Pentecost
Church	A	Ascension; 12th Pentecost; Christ the King
	B	2nd Epiphany; 13th Pentecost
	C	16th and 22nd Pentecost; All Saints Day
Comfort	A	2nd Easter
Commandments	A	6th Epiphany; Transfiguration; 16th Pentecost
	B	3rd Lent

Topic	Year	Sunday/Season
Communion (see Eucharist)		
Covenant	B	1st and 5th Lent
Creation/Creator	A	New Year's Eve; Pentecost; 1st Pentecost
	B	Pentecost
	C	5th Easter; 1st Pentecost
Deliverance	A	10th Pentecost
	B	3rd Advent; 15th Pentecost
Direction	B	1st Lent
	C	10th Pentecost
Diversity	A	Pentecost; 10th Pentecost
	B	2nd, 7th, 13th, and 19th Pentecost
	C	Pentecost; 4th and 10th Pentecost
Emmanuel	A	4th Advent; Christmas Eve
Endurance	A	Holy Week Wednesday
Eternal/Eternity	A	21st Pentecost
	B	2nd Advent; 7th Easter
Eucharist	A	Holy Week Thursday
Evangelism	B	3rd Epiphany; 3rd Pentecost
	C	5th Epiphany
Exile	C	20th Pentecost
Faith	A	2nd Lent; 2nd and 3rd Easter; 8th Pentecost
	B	9th Pentecost
	C	3rd and 19th Pentecost
Family	A	11th Pentecost
	B	8th Pentecost
Forgiveness	A	4th Advent; 2nd and 9th Pentecost
	B	3rd Easter; 11th Pentecost
	C	7th Epiphany; 4th Lent
Foundation	A	7th Epiphany
	B	2nd Epiphany
Freedom	A	Christmas Eve
	C	7th Easter

Topic	Year	Sunday/Season
Fruit	A	16th Pentecost
	C	6th Easter
Gifts	A	2nd Advent; Epiphany Sunday; 6th Easter; Pentecost
	B	1st Advent; 3rd and 25th Pentecost
	C	2nd and 8th Epiphany; 1st Lent; 6th Easter
Grace	A	2nd Christmas
	B	4th Lent; 6th Pentecost
	C	5th Epiphany
Growth	A	3rd Advent; Holy Week Monday
Guidance	A	Presentation/Candlemas
	B	1st Advent
Healing	A	3rd Advent
	B	5th and 6th Epiphany; 5th Pentecost
	C	6th Easter; 4th, 6th, and 13th Pentecost
Hope	A	5th Lent; Holy Week Monday; 3rd Easter
	B	3rd Advent; 4th Epiphany; 24th Pentecost
	C	4th Epiphany; 25th Pentecost
Hospitality	C	14th Pentecost
Inclusiveness	A	Christmas Eve; 2nd Christmas; 1st and 3rd Epiphany
	B	1st and 2nd Christmas; 2nd Epiphany; 2nd Lent; 5th Easter
	C	10th Pentecost; Thanksgiving
Invitation	A	2nd Advent
Joy	A	Christmas Day; 16th Pentecost
	B	3rd Advent; 4th and 6th Epiphany; 6th Pentecost
	C	3rd Advent; 5th Lent; 6th Easter; 6th Pentecost; Thanksgiving
Judgment	A	8th Epiphany; 13th and 22nd Pentecost
	C	7th and 11th Pentecost
Justice	A	5th Epiphany; 18th Pentecost
	B	23rd Pentecost
	C	8th Pentecost

Topic	Year	Sunday/Season
Law	A	7th Epiphany; 16th Pentecost
	B	2nd Christmas; 3rd Lent
	C	3rd Epiphany; 5th, 21st and 23rd Pentecost
Light	A	1st Advent; Christmas Eve; Christmas Day; 3rd, 4th, and 5th Epiphany; 4th Lent; Holy Week; Tuesday; 5th Easter; All Saints Day; 4th and 22nd Pentecost
	B	4th Lent; Transfiguration; 2nd Easter
	C	Transfiguration; 23rd Pentecost
Love	A	7th Epiphany; Easter; 6th and 19th Pentecost
	B	4th Lent; 4th and 5th Easter; 1st, 2nd and 3rd Pentecost
	C	1st and 2nd Advent; 4th and 7th Epiphany; 4th Lent; 5th Easter; 16th Pentecost
Meditation	C	4th Pentecost
Ministry	C	2nd and 4th Epiphany; 6th Pentecost
Mission	A	Ash Wednesday
	B	4th, 5th, 6th, and 7th Easter; 5th, 6th, 14th, and 15th Pentecost
	C	3rd Advent; 2nd, 3rd, and 5th Epiphany; 25th Pentecost
Music	A	2nd and 3rd Advent; Christmas Eve; 2nd Epiphany; Holy Week Thursday; 13th and 20th Pentecost
	B	2nd Christmas
	C	8th Epiphany; Ascension; 2nd and 25th Pentecost
Names of Christ	A	4th Advent
Patience	A	8th Pentecost
	B	1st Advent

Topic	Year	Sunday/Season
Peace	A	1st and 2nd Advent; 1st Epiphany; 2nd Easter
	B	2nd Advent; 1st Epiphany; 17th and 23rd Pentecost
	C	1st and 7th Epiphany; 6th Easter
Perseverance	A	8th Pentecost
	C	22nd Pentecost
Planning	C	15th Pentecost
Praise	A	1st Christmas; 3rd Easter
	B	1st Christmas; 4th Epiphany
	C	1st Christmas; 20th Pentecost; All Saints Day
Prayer	A	Ash Wednesday; 7th Easter; 17th Pentecost; All Saints Day
	B	3rd Advent; 9th and 18th Pentecost
	C	3rd Advent; 9th, 17th, and 23rd Pentecost; All Saints Day
Prophecy	A	1st Epiphany; 2nd Easter
	B	4th Advent
	C	1st, 2nd, and 4th Advent; 22nd Pentecost
Protection	A	2nd Lent; Holy Week Tuesday; 7th Easter
	B	13th Pentecost
	C	2nd Lent; 18th Pentecost
Provision	A	14th Pentecost
Readiness	A	21st Pentecost
	C	11th Pentecost
Reconciliation	A	6th Epiphany; 9th Pentecost
Redemption	A	Christmas Eve
	B	5th and 11th Pentecost
Remnant/Chosen	A	New Year's Eve; 2nd Epiphany; 4th Lent
Repentance	A	Ash Wednesday
Restoration	C	9th Pentecost
Resurrection	A	5th Lent; Easter
	B	2nd Easter
	C	Easter; 2nd, 12th and 24th Pentecost

Topic	Year	Sunday/Season
Revelation	A	3rd Easter
	C	2nd Pentecost
Righteousness	A	2nd Advent; 4th Epiphany; 7th Pentecost
	B	1st Christmas
	C	1st Advent
Sacrifice	A	Holy Week Monday
	B	21st, 23rd, and 24th Pentecost; Christ the King
	C	4th Advent
Salvation	A	Christmas Eve; 8th Epiphany; Holy Week Saturday; 9th Pentecost
	B	4th Advent; 3rd Epiphany
	C	Christ the King Sunday
Seek	A	2nd Epiphany; 22nd Pentecost
Servanthood	A	New Year's Eve/Day; Ash Wednesday, Holy Week Thursday and Saturday; 3rd, 15th, and 21st Pentecost; Christ the King
	B	5th Lent; 9th Pentecost
	C	14th and 25th Pentecost
Sins	A	Ash Wednesday; 3rd Pentecost
	B	5th Lent; 3rd Easter
	C	16th Pentecost
Spirit	A	6th Easter; 4th and 14th Pentecost
	B	1st Epiphany; 4th and 7th Easter; Pentecost
	C	1st Epiphany; Pentecost; 1st Pentecost
Spiritual Growth	A	6th Epiphany
Story	A	15th Pentecost
	C	8th, 20th, and 24th Pentecost
Strength	A	2nd Epiphany
	C	2nd Lent; 14th Pentecost
Stumbling Block	B	4th Epiphany; 4th and 18th Pentecost
Teacher	A	Palm/Passion; Holy Week Wednesday; 20th Pentecost
	B	8th Pentecost
Temptation	A	1st Lent
	C	1st Lent

Topic	Year	Sunday/Season
Thanksgiving	A, B, C	5th and 20th Pentecost
Thirst	A	3rd Lent; 2nd Pentecost
Time	A	New Year's Eve/Day
	C	Ascension
Trust	A	2nd Pentecost
	B	3rd Easter
Unity	A	Easter; 7th Easter; Pentecost; 9th Pentecost; All Saints Day
	B	1st, 2nd, and 7th Pentecost; 2nd Easter; 7th and 19th Pentecost
	C	5th and 7th Easter; 4th and 10th Pentecost
Waiting	B	1st and 2nd Advent
	C	11th and 23rd Pentecost
Warning	C	12th Pentecost
Watchfulness (attention)	A	1st Lent
Wind	B	Pentecost
Wisdom	A	5th Epiphany
	B	12th and 16th Pentecost
Witness	A	2nd Easter; 19th Pentecost
	B	3rd Epiphany; 5th Easter; 3rd Pentecost
	C	2nd and 6th Easter; 7th and 24th Pentecost
Works	A	6th Easter; 1st Pentecost

SCRIPTURE INDEX

CPSIA information can be obtained at www.ICGtesting.com
Printed in the USA
LVOW011638160812

294618LV00002B/4/P